Economics

Economics

Productivity and Technology Shocks

Guthlac N.Kirk Anyalezu, Ph.D.

authorHOUSE®

AuthorHouse™
1663 Liberty Drive
Bloomington, IN 47403
www.authorhouse.com
Phone: 1 (800) 839-8640

Published by AuthorHouse 04/30/2015

ISBN: 978-1-5049-0317-2 (sc)
ISBN: 978-1-5049-0318-9 (hc)
ISBN: 978-1-5049-0316-5 (e)

Library of Congress Control Number: 2015905611

About the Author

Guthlac N. Kirk Anyalezu is Professor of Economics at the University of Phoenix and Austin Community College. He is a Business Development Analyst at Capital City Mortgage, Austin Texas. Professor Anyalezu has been Visiting Professor at Devry University and Keller Graduate Management School, Houston.

He has received numerous awards for Research and Scholarship and Honorarium awards from the University of Phoenix in 2010, 2011, 2013, and 2014. In 2011, he received the University of Phoenix Business School Faculty Leadership Award. He is a Faculty Research and Scholarship Colloquium leader at the University.

His research and publications focus on measuring Total Factor Productivity, Technology Shocks, Real Business Cycle Models, and on Accounting and Banking Regulatory Controls. He has contributed to two books in Accounting and Economics.

Professor Anyalezu has a BA (Combined Honors) in Accounting and Economics from Metropolitan University London, M.Sc in Economics Birkbeck College, University of London, M.Phil. in Economics from SOAS, University of London and Ph.D. in Economics from University of Surrey.

He is a member of the Royal Economics Society; member of the American Association of International Researcher; Academic member of Athens Institute of Education and Research – Economics Research Unit; Accounting and Finance Research Unit; Associate member of the Chartered Institute of Bankers; the Chartered Association of Certified Accountants. He is also a member of the Association of Business Executives; the Institute of Administrative Management, and the British Institute of Management.

Professor Anyalezu is the Editor-in-Chief of the Journal of Economics and Development Studies, American Research Institute for Policy Development and Editorial Board member. He is a member of the Editorial and Reviewers Board of the Athens Journal of Business and Economics.

To my Family

Abstract

This book is essentially an advanced econometrics focused on the empirical estimation of total factor productivity (TFP) and technology shocks or contractionary effects. The findings showed no significant evidence of contractionary effects on the UK private business economy on aggregate level. On disaggregate sectoral level; there were some evidence of contractionary effects, emanating from the non-durable sectors and non-manufacturing sectors. Given that the research is an applied econometrics, the book therefore, utilised various methodologies to estimate TFP and technology shocks. Equally, it uses two identifying approaches to measure technology. The study employs the latest state of the art techniques in econometric modelling. This is also the first major empirical research focused on analysing technological impact responses to hours or employment for the whole of UK economy sectors at aggregate and disaggregates level.

The motivating objective is a focus on the underlying influential factors associated with real business cycles model predictions. To perform the task of investigating technological innovation the study uses the UK manufacturing sectors and the impact on hours worked or employment. I made use of annual data, as well as quarterly data for the period 1969 – 2006.

The book is structure into six chapters. Each chapter dealt with the specifics of the methodologies relevant to that particular empirical analysis. The adoption and construction of four distinct models for the study facilitated the establishment of each area of investigation and their inter-relationships. This makes it very useful for applications to both microeconomic and macroeconomic strategy and policy inferences. This book will be of interest and will serve as a useful tool to government policy makers, central banks and other financial institutions, and/or industrial organizations and academics. This is especially its importance for monetary policy implications. This book will be a good companion to university students, especially graduate students undertaking advanced econometrics.

Gathac Kirk Nkem Anyalezu, Ph.D

Acknowledgments

The process toward this book would not have been possible without the kind assistance of some wonderful individuals.

First, I would like to thank unreservedly my wife, Chibuzor, my children, Zizi Sarah, Zara Mya, and Zoey Mckayla. Thanks to my mum and dad, Sarah Bernadette and Sir Justin A. Anyalezu. Thanks to my family, Kentigern, Joy Lawrentia, Teddy, Ursula, Obia, Ngozi, Chidi, Chinwe, Ash Okoro and my friend Jane F. Lambert for all their affectionate support, patience and encouragements.

I would like to thank Ali Choudhary and Vasco Gabriel for advice during the course of research. I am greatly indebted to John Fernald (Federal Reserve Bank of San Francisco and University of Chicago). Fernald assistance with the BFK dataset, advice on the difficulties of measuring TFP and explanations to my inquiring questions are indeed invaluable. It would not have been possible to complete this research without the generosity of responses to my requests.

I am grateful to Nicholas Oulton and Sally Srinivasan (both of the Bank of England) for responding to my request for data. I am indeed grateful to Kim Pompilii and to the Bank of England for granting me non-exclusive world rights to use the Bank of England Industry Dataset. The BEID made it possible to conduct this research for the UK economy. My thanks also go to the National Office of Statistics

(UK), especially to Alyson Box for fantastic assistance with data access. In addition, I would like to thank Jordi Gali (New York University), for his response to my request.

Finally, I would like to thank all my friends and all those that gave assistance in one way or the other through the course of this research. This is especially, to the University of Surrey Librarian for facilitating access to the OECD database request.

Guthlac Kirk Nkem Anyalezu, Ph.D

Contents

About the Author v

Abstract ix

Acknowledgments xi

Contents xiii

List of Figures xvii

List of Tables xix

Econometric Packages Used xxi

Chapter 1   Introduction and Literature Review 1

1.0   Introduction 1

1.0a: The Research Questions 2

1.1:   Literature Review 3

1.2   The Definitions and Explanations of TFP and
         RBC Models 6

1.2.1   Total Factor Productivity Definition 6

1.2.1A: The Model: 8

1.2.2   RBC Model Definition 9

1.2.3   The Background 20

1.3.   RBC Model, Technology Shocks and
         Aggregate Fluctuations 22

1.3.1   The Solow Residual as Proxy to Technology 23

1.3.2   Labor – Hoarding, Productivity and True
         Technology Shocks 24

1.3.3:   The Invariance Properties of Solow's
         Productivity Residual 25

1.3.4   The Novelty of RBC Models 27

1.3.5   Perceptions on Testing 31

1.3.6   The Impulse Mechanism 32

1.3.7   The Propagation Mechanism 32

1.3.8	Neutrality to logarithm level or first difference approach	34
1.4	Conclusions	47
1.6	The Aims and Scope of the Study	49
1.7	The Book Organisation	50

Chapter 2   The Estimation of Aggregate Productivity and Aggregate Technology 53

2.0	Introduction	53
2.1	The Model Specification	54
2.2	The Aggregation over Firms Specification	59
2.3.1	The implications of the markup terms	61
2.3.2.	The Welfare Implication	61
2.4	Data Analysis and methodology	65
2.4.1	Data	66
2.4.1A.	Output: Nominal output	66
2.4.1B	Capital	68
2.4.2	The Method	69
2.4.3	Labour	71
2.4.4	Intermediate input	72
2.4.5.	The Instrumental variables	72
2.5	The Empirical Results	75
2.6	Conclusions	81
	Appendix to chapter 2	84
	Appendix A2.1	84
	Appendix A2.2: The Divisia Index	85

Chapter 3   The Aggregate Productivity, Technology and Contractionary Effects 92

3.0	Introduction	92
3.1	The Implications for Real Business Cycles (RBC)	94
3.2.	The Model Approach	96
3.3	Results	99
3.4	Conclusions	111

Chapter 4	**Technology Shocks and Aggregate Fluctuations** **115**	
4.1	Introduction 115	
4.2	The Model – First Approach (Gali, (1999)) 119	
4.2.1	The Specification and Conditional Correlation Estimators 122	
4.3	The Alternative Methodological Approach 123	
4.3.1	Explanation of the VAR Model 127	
4.4	Data Analysis and Hours Stationarity Test 129	
4.4.1	Data and Variables Definitions 130	
4.4.2	Variables definition - Bivariate model 133	
4.5	The Empirical Findings and Results 137	
4.6	The Evidence from a Five-Variable Model 142	
4.6.1	Results 143	
4.6.2	Additional Analysis 144	
4.7	Conclusions 149	
	Appendix to chapter 4: Model approach 152	
A4.2.1:	The Households Factor: 152	
A4.2.2:	The Firms Level Factor 153	
A4.2.3:	The Monetary Policy Factor 154	
A4.2.4:	The Equilibrium Factor 154	
Chapter 5	**Technological Innovations in the UK Private Business Economy: The Effects on Employment and Sectoral Level Estimations 161**	
5.0	Introduction 161	
5.1	Technological Innovations 162	
5.2	The empirical methodology 164	
5.2.1	Data 164	
5.3	Permanent Technology Shocks Identification 165	
5.4	The Methodology 166	
5.5	The Results 168	
5.6	The Sticky Price Issue 188	
5.7	Labor Productivity and TFP Growth Shocks 189	

5.4   Conclusions 194

Appendix 197

A5.1   Econometric Tests: Endogeneity........................... 197

A5.2.1:   The Fixed Effect Models..................................... 199

A5.3:   The Testing For Endogeneity Methodology 202

A5.3.1:   The Testing Approach... 203

A5.3.2   Testing for Endogeneity of a Single Explanatory
              Variable... 204

Chapter 6   **Concluding Remarks 207**

6.1:   The Empirical Research Findings 207

6.2   Summary Conclusions 210

Bibliography.. 215

List of Figures

Chapter 1

Figure 1.1: An Abstract Real Business Cycle............................10

Figure 1.2: Technology Shock and Labor market 13

Chapter 2

Figure 2.1: The Estimated UK Productivity and
Technology Growth Rates 76

Figure 2.2: The Level of TFP in U.K: Aggregate
Productivity and Aggregate Technology
(normalised to one in 1970) 77

Chapter 3

Figure 3.1: Aggregate productivity and Technology................99

A: UK private business economy with hours........100

B: Private business economy without hours 100

C: Prod, Tech and Tech hours (Private
Economy) 101

D: TFP whole Economy with Tech hours............ 101

E: Percent changes in TFP, Output & Hours 102

F: Changes between private & manufacturing..... 102

Figure 3.2: Aggregate Productivity and Technology
percentage change in UK manufacturing
sector (A) and B, the private economy. 104

Figure 3.2 (c): Aggregate Productivity Manufacturing
and the whole economy 105

Figure 3.3: Aggregate Productivity and Technology in
manufacturing sector 106

Chapter 4

Figure 4.1a UK: Stationarity - hours 132

Figure 4.1b Stationarity- hours...132

Figure 4.1C: The Different Hours Series 132

Figure 4.2: Productivity and Employment 139

Figure 4.3: Impulse Responses Bivariate Model – de-
trended hours 140

Figure 4.4 - 4.6: Impulse responses to level specification:
Bivariate hours.. 146

Figure 4.7 – 4.8: Impulse Responses for Log and First
Difference Levels Multiple and Combined
Graphs.. 147

Figure 4.9 – 4.10 Impulse Responses First Difference Level 148

Figure 4.11a: Productivity and Employment....................... 151

Figure 4.11b: Combined Responses 151

Chapter 5

Figure 5.1a: Aggregates Manufacturing Impulse Responses... 169

Figure 5.1 b – c: Aggregates Manufacturing Impulse
Responses 170

Figure 5.2c – d: Impulse Response Manufacturing Sector..... 193

List of Tables

Chapter 1

Table 1.0 Summaries of Literatures Reviewed:
Technology Shocks & aggregate Fluctuations 37

Table 1.2: Summaries of Reviewed Papers: Technology
Shocks & Aggregate Fluctuations 47

Chapter 2

Table 2.1: Sectoral Estimated Markups (1970 – 2000)
– U.K 80

Table 2.2: List of industries and their definitions – U.K..........83

Chapter 3

Table 3.1: Summary of the Mean and Standard
Deviation of TFP 107

Table 3.2: Regressions on Current and Lagged
Technology..109

Table 3.3: Sectoral Estimated Markups for the U.K
Private Business Economy.....................................110

Table 3.4: U.K Manufacturing Sectors Markups (1970
– 2000)... 111

Chapter 4

Table 4.1: Unit Root Test on $(\Delta M 0)$ 136

Table 4.2: Bivariate Estimations (SVAR): Correlations..........138

Table 4.3: Five-Variable Model: Estimates 143

Table 4.4: The Augmented Dickey-Fuller (ADF) Unit
Root ADF Test..144

Chapter 5

Table 5.1: Excluded Sectors 165

Table 5.2:   Regressions on current and lagged (TFP)
technology shocks Δt 171

Table 5.2.1: Industries showing Contractionary Effect by
Sectors 174
Table 5.3.1 Conditional Correlation Estimates:
TFP/ Hours 175
Table 5.3.2 Conditional Correlation Estimates:
TFP/ LAB 177
Table 5.3.3 Conditional Correlation Estimates:
TFP/ LABQA 179
Table 5.4.1 Conditional Correlation Estimates:
BFK Hours 181
Table 5.4.2 Conditional Correlation Estimates:
BFK LAB 183
Table 5.4.3 Conditional Correlation Estimates:
BFK LABQA 185

Econometric Packages Used

Eviews 5.0 & 5.1
Gauss
Other Software: Microsoft Excel

Data Sources:
Bank of England (BEID)
BFK Dataset (2002)
Hendry Dataset – Oxford
Jenkins Defence
IEA
International Monetary Fund – International Financial Statistics Dataset
(IMF – IFS)
OECD
Office of National Statistics (ONS)
OPEC
SPIRI
World Bank

Chapter 1

Introduction and Literature Review

1.0   Introduction

This introductory chapter provides the literature review and the scope of the book. The theme is to provide for the objective to demonstrate the significant role of technology shocks and hours worked and/or employment. A fundamental aim in this book is the examination of the issues involved including the approaches to estimating Total Factor Productivity (TFP hereafter). It investigates the relationship between technology and hours worked or employment. The other ambition for this chapter is to provide a comprehensive background about the estimation techniques used in the empirical chapters.

The structure and organization of this chapter is in sections as follows. Section 1.0a discusses the questions this book sets out to provide some insights. Section1.1 is the literatures review. In section 1.2, provides the definitions associated with TFP and real business cycle (RBC hereafter) models. Section 1.3 examines the RBC theory, technology shocks and aggregate fluctuations, including historical development of the model. Section 1.4 is on the economic growth theory, which consists of a review on the neoclassical and endogenous growth models. Section 1.5, is the conclusion to this chapter while section 1.6, provide the explanations to the aims and scope of the book, and section 1.7, gives an overview on the organisation of the book.

1.0a: The Research Questions

The overriding focus of this book is to determine what happens when technology improves and the effects on productivity and employment or hours worked. In other words, to test the hypothesis that following a positive technology shocks, total hours worked rises. Therefore, the ultimate aim of the book is to provide answers to a comprehensive set of questions. The salient research questions are as follows

1) Does a difference exist between aggregate productivity and aggregate Technology? This question explores the difference between the two (aggregate productivity and aggregate technology), which if it does exist will be due to increased efficiency or improvement in technology.

2) Taking into consideration the role of total factor productivity (TFP), is controlling for imperfect competition important in estimating TFP? This question relates to the need to find an appropriate method of estimating accurately TFP. This is because firms differ in various ways and it is difficult for firms to compete equally, hence the need to use a proxy variable that will capture the control for imperfect competition.

3) From the estimations of aggregate technology shocks, are there any findings or evidence of contractionary effects after a positive technology shocks, using the UK economy or the UK private business economy as a case study? The intention for this question is to either ascertain evidence if any exists of contraction at the aggregate or disaggregate sectors following a positive technology shocks. It also investigates if productivity and hours worked rises or falls after a positive technology shocks in the economy.

4) Finally the big question which is, are the empirical results or findings in this book in conformity or compliance with the RBC model predictions? In addition, it is to determine if the empirical findings are of the same views as that postulation by RBC theories.

5) is necessary given the book hypothesis and the objective of finding out what happens when technology improves or innovates.

In this book, I used first, the growth accounting model and secondly the structural vector autoregressive model. The first methodological approach measures technology directly. The second methodology measures technology through imposing a restriction on the long run impulse responses. For both methodologies, a great detailed data were required. Therefore, owning to data availability the book concentrated only on the UK economy as a case study. Furthermore, the book uses applied econometrics modelling to address all the above questions.

The next section of this chapter is on the literature review in relation to the questions posed in this book.

1.1:   Literature Review

There is an increasing amount of literature on total factor productivity (TFP) and the real business cycle (RBC) model. The attempt in this book is to provide a comprehensive literature survey that relates to both TFP and RBC models, Anyalezu, (2014). The reference to RBC model is important because of its predictions on the effects of technology improvement and/or innovations on hours worked or employment after a positive technology shocks. For RBC, one can begin by examining the seminal works of Kydland and Prescott (1982, 1990), Lucas (1977, 1980), Long and Plosser (1983), Mankiw (1989), McCallum (1989), Plosser (1989), Stadler (1994), Cooley (1995), King, Plosser and Rebelo

(1988), King and Rebelo (2000). This is just to name a few leading RBC theorist.

In terms of the TFP, the empirical task of modelling it at aggregate and firm level for the U.K or indeed any economy is a complicated process. The reason is because TFP can act as the source of the cause as well as the consequence of the evolution of dynamic system operating in the economy for example, technical progress, accumulation of capital, enterprise and institutional arrangements (Nadiri (1970)). Therefore, to measure and explain its behaviour at the microeconomic and macroeconomic levels will require the dismantling of many complex factors.

In the RBC theory, many studies assume that technological shocks are an influential source of business cycle volatility. For example, RBC model emphasizes supply or technology disturbances as the main source of macroeconomic fluctuations in a world with rational firms (individuals)[1] and perfectly flexible prices. The theoretical approach stance is an adoption of better-than-average growth in the economy's technological capability, which induces firms to invest in new resources like plants and equipment, at a faster-than-average rate. With an increase in investment, the demand for investment goods and employment growth rises. This in turn leads to faster-than-average growth in consumer spending (see for example, Tang (2002)). Equally, see as an example Kydland and Prescott (1991) estimation` of the variations in Solow technology parameter as a source of aggregate fluctuations, with the finding that it could account for about 70 percept of the variance in US post-war cyclical fluctuations.

---

[1] Begg, Fischer, and Dornbusch, (1994), provided good interpretations of the terms trade, individual and business cycles. Trade in Victorian time refers to industry while individual means firms. In UK, short run fluctuations are referred to as trade cycles while for the Americans the term business cycles are used. However, modern economists now use the term business cycle.

TFP therefore, following the outline above, can determine labour productivity through capital per employee. The approach usually employed to measure TFP has been to distinguish between shifts in aggregate production function. In other words, measuring technical change and the activities on production function and factor accumulation (see for example Hulten, 1975)[2]. There have been an adoption of several approaches have over time been adopted to explain the distinctions in long-run economic performance. For example, the application of the Solow (1957) productivity analysis to differences in levels of output per worker across countries (Hall & Jones (1996))[3]. To explain economic improvement, the GDP growth rate is often used. The pitfall with it is that it tends to overstate the improvement in economic welfare. The reason is due to the failure to measure the depletion of natural resources and the negative spillover externalities that associate with rapid GDP growth rate (see for example Hulten (2000))[4]. It is imperative because of the stated implications, to find a method that can measure TFP and the shocks to the economy as accurately as possible.

The TFP estimations in this book adopts as closely as possible the approaches advocated by Basu and Fernald ((BF), 1997, 2002, and BFK 2004), as well as paying particular attention to Hall (1986, 1988). For technology shocks, I employ three different approaches, namely, Gali (1999) and Christiano, Eichenbaum and Vigfusson ((2003), will be referred to as CEV hereafter), Chang and Hong (CH (2006)). By making use of the general accounting framework, it is possible to identify the gap between productivity and technology. Equally, productivity at some interval periods may lie above technology and vice versa. Where this occurs, the interpretation or assumption is that, the gaps between them reflect friction in output and factor markets.

---

[2] See also, Christensen, L and Jorgenson, D (1970), Denison, E (1972), and Jorgenson, D and Griliches, Z (1972a, b).

[3] Hall, R.E and Jones, C.I. (1996) 'The productivity of Nations', NBER Working Paper Series 5812

[4] Hulten, C (2000), 'Total factor productivity: A short biography', NBER.

For example, Lipsey and Carlaw (2000), revised (2001), assesses the contributory qualities of TFP and the extent to which it represents the measure of an economy's technological change or dynamism and the interrelationships that underline the process of long-term growth. On this note, the next section examines some conceptual definitions with current TFP and RBC measurements.

1.2   The Definitions and Explanations of TFP and RBC Models

This section examines the definitions of TFP and RBC models. It also provides explanations to both models respectively.

1.2.1   Total Factor Productivity Definition

Productivity is a key performance benchmark and has profound implications for industrial and regulatory policies such as central banks, investment banks and governments. Therefore, rising productivity relates to increased profitability, lower costs and sustained competitiveness. For firms, the most commonly used productivity indicator is labour productivity, that is, units of output or value added per employee. Of course, this measure has some drawbacks of which the most important one is the failure to show the reason labour productivity has risen. An example would be to compare say, labour productivity in investment banks outpacing the overall economy.

A possible question therefore would be, is it because of increased investment in technology or is it because of economies of scale such as improved efficiency or downsizing or mergers? To derive the solution to these questions, we can utilize the Solow model. The reason is because; Solow (1957) found that many countries economic growth was attributable to "technical change", or "total factor productivity growth". Thus, the proposal to measure as a "residual" based on "production function approach".

Since then, the production function approach has been used a lot to measure the rate of return to net investment in research and development (R&D) for firms (Griliches (1986)) and industry aggregates (Griliches (1979, 1994), Griliches and Lichtenberg (1984), Scherer (1982)). In addition, the importance of TFP makes it necessary for continuous introduction of improvements into the methods of measurements. For example, in considering the returns to scale (RTS hereafter) and TFP, Caves, Christensen and Swanson ((1981), hereafter CCS) proposed estimating a variable cost function rather than a total cost function when the sample contains firms that are unable to fully adjust some of their inputs to optimal levels in each time period. There has been application of the CCS approach to empirical measurement of scale economies in the presence of quasi-fixed inputs (Oum, Tretheway and Zhang (1991)).

Total factor productivity (TFP) is widely used in both macroeconomic and microeconomic studies and is often refers to as multiple or joint factor productivity (MFP). The concept of TFP together with the fact that labour is not the only factor of production but also includes entrepreneur ability, land and capital are important in considering productivity measurement. In addition, the discussion around the subject started as far back as the 1930s and subsequently led to the establishment of TFP measurement and growth accounting (see Griliches (1995))[5]. Nevertheless, using Solow's approach and the hypothesis of TFP as a microeconomic tool it may be feasible to analyse and differentiate labour productivity change at firm level. In addition, it can indicate whether firm level labour productivity gains are determined principally by capital investment or by technology and knowledge.

---

[5] According to Griliches, (1995), some of the early studies on TFP measurement commenced with the output-over-input in Copeland (1937) to its codification in Solow (1957). Other studies include those by Tinbergen (1942), Stigler (1947), Schmookler (1952), Fabricant (1954), Kendrick (1955 and 1956), and Abramovitz (1956).

The conventional definition of TFP defines it; "as the residual growth of real product not accounted for by the growth of real factor input" (see Hulten (1978)). In other words, it represents and/or explains that part of output growth not accounted for by the growth in inputs. In addition, it implies a reflection of the productivity of all inputs in producing an output. For example, if we assume there are only two categories of inputs, capital and labor, TFP is the weighted average of capital and labor productivity, adjusted for the additional input available due to increased factor efficiency.

To illustrate TFP, we can create a very simple model. The basic principles from this will apply in developing the TFP estimation model in chapters 2 and 3 of this book. For understanding the derivation or estimation of TFP, this basic model will suffice for now.

1.2.1A: The Model:

A simple model derivation will show TFP as:

$$TFP = VA / (K^{1-\alpha} L^{\alpha})$$

$\hspace{10cm}$ (1.1)

Where: TFP is Total Factor Productivity, VA is the Value Added; K denotes Capital and L represents the Number of Employees, or Total Annual Labor Hours or Hours Worked. The term α is a fraction or share of VA attributable to labor.

Thus $\alpha = L(VMP_L) / VA$, where VMP_L is the value of the marginal product of labor and, the term $1-\alpha$ is a fraction of value added attributable to capital.

Equally, $1-\alpha = L(VMP_K) / VA$ where VMP_K is the value of the marginal product of capital, and therefore, dividing through by L yields the expression:

$$TFP = \frac{(VA/L)}{[(K/L)^{1-\alpha}}$$ (1.2)

In which case, taking the logarithms of both sides of the equation (1.2) would provide the expression:

$$\log(TFP) = \log(VA/L) - (1-\alpha)\log[K/L]/t$$ (1.3)

Furthermore, by differentiating with respect to time $(\delta/\delta t)$:

$$\delta \log(TFP)/\delta t = \delta \log[VA/L]/\delta t - (1-\alpha)\delta \log[K/L]/\delta t$$ (1.4)

Equation (1.4) means that the percentage change in TFP is equal to the percentage change in value added per employee less $(1-\alpha)$ (the percentage change in capital per employee).

The model derivation therefore implies that, the change in TFP when computed for individual firms or firm level will show the underlying factors that determines labor productivity. Thus, TFP in this case provides a method to quantify the contributions to growth of the different factors (Stiglitz and Driffill (2000)). Thus, a rising TFP can relate directly to higher output; and as such, act as an essential tool for measuring economic progress. Having considered the definition of TFP, we can proceed to consider the RBC models.

1.2.2 RBC Model Definition

Real business cycle (RBC) model and the term economic cycle are different things.

The term economic cycle is by definition a periodic fluctuation of economic activities especially with respect to its long-term growth trend.

The cycle represents a shift over time between periods of relatively rapid growth of output, commonly referred to as recovery or boom and periods of relative stagnation or decline, implying a contraction or recession as depicted in figure 1.1 below. The measure of these fluctuations usually uses the real gross domestic product (RGDP), while the government role in this is to smooth out the business cycle and control or reduce its fluctuations.

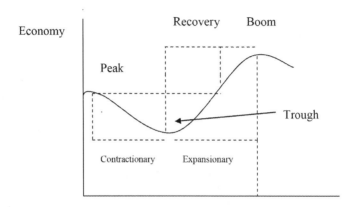

Figure 1.1: An Abstract Real Business Cycle

In view of the fact that the cycles do not tend to repeat at regular time intervals, their lengths or peak to peak, or from trough to trough as in figure 1.1. The most important concern is whether similar mechanisms that generate recessions and/or expansions that exist in the economies for the dynamics that appears as a cycle if they can occur repeatedly. See for example, Burns and Mitchell (1946), Sorensen and Whitta-Jacobsen (2005) on business cycles. According to Long and Plosser (1983), "business cycle refers to joint time-series behavior of a wide range of economic variables such as prices, output, employment and investment. In actual economies, this behavior seems to be characterised by at least two broad regularities:

1) Measured as deviations from trend, the up and down in individual series exhibit a considerable amount of persistence.
2) Measures of various economic activities (e.g. outputs in different sectors) move together".

Therefore, for the purpose of this book, I define "contractionary effects" as a contraction arising due to technology shocks and price stickiness. The contractionary effect of technology shocks will be much stronger for firms with stickier prices.

See for example, Marchetti and Nucci (2005) analysis on the Italian manufacturing. The basis for the RBC models evaluation is on their ability to match patterns of co-movements observed in the data of selected macroeconomic variables. A few recent studies indicate evidence of a correlation between technology shocks and labor input. In particular, Basu and Fernald (BF, (1997)) and Gali (1999), reported on the negative correlation between technology shocks, identified under different assumptions and several measures of labor and other inputs. The interpretation of the findings, are difficult to reconcile with predictions of standard flexible-price model, as evidence in favor of sticky price models.

Gali (1999) on the other hand, showed that in a model economy with sticky prices and a money supply less than fully responsive to technology shocks, a technology innovation has a negative short run effect on hours. Further more, in the rise of a technology expansion nominal rigidities prevent prices from falling and thus aggregate demand does not increase. Thus, firms produce the same amount of output with a smaller volume of inputs, which have become more productive. A few studies supported Gali, by suggesting that the results depend on the response of the monetary authorities to technology shocks.

On the other hand, Dotsey, (2002), for example, shows that if the central bank follows the optimal monetary policy or a Taylor rule, (1993), or Clarida et al., (2000), then the effect of technology shocks on employment is no longer negative. This is because monetary policy by responding to deviations of inflation from target and to deviations of output from its natural level would reduce the policy rate to accommodate the shock fully. As a result, with these specifications of monetary policy, sticky and flexible price models would be observationally equivalent with respect to the predicted co-movement of productivity and labor and no inference on the prevailing price setting behavior to obtain from the data.

However, according to Lucas (1977), business cycles are an attempt to construct a model in the most literal sense: "a fully articulated artificial economy which behaves through time so as to imitate closely the time series behaviour of actual economies. In addition, Keynes through the "General Theory" attempted to achieve this explicitness and empirical accuracy that the RBC model advocates. The concern of these models to imitate actual economies has been on the ability to make accurate conditional forecasts, to evaluate how behavior would have differed had certain policies been different in specified ways, Anyalezu (2013). Therefore, we can investigate this in more detail by categorizing technology shocks into two forms: transitory (purely temporary) shocks and a permanent shock.

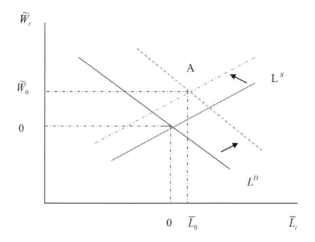

Figure 1.2: Technology Shock and Labor market

A Transitory (temporary) shock ($\rho z = 0$)

To illustrate the exposition, I adopt here the approaches by Heijdra and Van der Ploeg (2002), King, and Rebelo (1999) by considering the effects of a temporary shock with a labor market and technology shock as depicted in figure 1.2 above. The assumption is that the shock does not exhibit any serial correlation, hence $\rho z = 0$. Equally, through the assumption it is feasible for the response to technology shock to be represented as $\tilde{Z}_t = \varepsilon_t^z$ and $\tilde{Z}_t = 0$ for t = 1, 2... It therefore, implies that with the transitory shock there is no long-run effect on the macro economy. Moreover, this is because technology only deviates in the impact period from its steady state level. However, the effect on consumption and other variables are non-zero. Therefore, the consumption function with a transitory shock is as follows:

$$\tilde{C}_t = \frac{\phi[\lambda_2 + \varsigma(\phi - 1)]\varepsilon_t^z}{(\lambda_2 + \varsigma)[\omega_c + \phi - 1]} > 0. \tag{1.5}$$

Where ρz is the autoregressive parameter, Z_t is the general productivity parameter, ρ is a pure rate of time preference. In the above equation (1.5), $\tilde{C}_t$ denotes consumption (leisure), ϕ is instantaneous utility (or felicity), representing the parameter for the effects of inter-temporal substitution in labor supply, in which case $1 \le \phi = \frac{1+\omega_{LL}}{1+\omega_{LL}(1-\varepsilon_L)} < \frac{1}{1-\varepsilon_L}$. The term ς represents the output effect and as such satisfies $0 < \varsigma(\phi-1) < 1$ while the term λ_2 denotes the unstable (positive) characteristic root of Δ_I, i.e. $\lambda_2 > 0$., the term $\omega_C = C/Y$, and is the output share of private consumption. Finally, $\omega_{LL} = (1-L)/L$ and implies that the wage elasticity of labor supply is given by $\sigma_L \omega_{LL}$, representing the ratio between leisure and labor. For any given ω_{LL} the elasticity rises with σ_L, also, ε_L represents the efficiency parameter of labor.

Equation (1.5) above implies that consumption will rise during the impact period due to technology shock despite the fact it may be for a short term. In which case, it will imply that, agents or a representative firm (household) will become richer. This is especially more so given that, leisure such as consumption is a normal good and as such, the shock can and/or is capable of causing a wealth effect in labor supply. In figure 1.2, the labor supply curve shifts up to the left. Instantaneously, the shock raises labor productivity thus labor demand. Under this scenario, irrespective of the capital stock being predetermined in the impact period, the labor demand curve shifts up and to the right.

The impact effect on the wage rate is unambiguously positive, while the effect on employment appears to be ambiguous. The reason is due to the dependency on the relative magnitudes of the labor supply and demand effects. Therefore, from equation (1.5) and $\tilde{Z}_t = \varepsilon_t^z$, the analytical expression for $\tilde{L}_t$ (labor), $\tilde{W}_t$ (real wage), and   (output) would yield to the following expressions:

$$\tilde{L}_t = \left(\frac{\phi-1}{\varepsilon_L}\right)\left[1 - \frac{\phi[\lambda_2 + \varsigma(\phi-1]}{(1+\lambda_2)[\omega_C + \phi - 1]}\right]\varepsilon_t^z, \tag{1.6}$$

$$\tilde{W}_t = \left[\frac{1-\phi(1-\varepsilon_L)}{\varepsilon_L}\right]\varepsilon_t^z + \left[\frac{(\phi-1)(1-\varepsilon_L)}{\varepsilon_L}\right]\tilde{C}_t > 0, \tag{1.7}$$

$$\tilde{Y}_t = \left[\frac{(1-\lambda_2)\omega_C + (\phi-1)[1-\varsigma(\phi-1)]}{(1+\lambda_2)[\omega_C + \phi - 1]}\right]\phi\varepsilon_t^z > 0. \tag{1.8}$$

On the other hand, (Heijdra et al, (2002)), using a calibration approach showed that the labor-demand effect (revenue side) would dominate the labor-supply effect (cost side), such that employment increases in the impact period as demonstrated in figure 1.2. In addition, the wage rate increases on impact irrespective of the parameter values as the labor-demand and supply effects co-move in the same direction. Although employment effect is ambiguous, output effect is unambiguously positive. Further more, given that output rises and capital is predetermined at impact, the immediate effect on the interest rate is positive, while the impact effect on investment is derived from equation (1.5) and setting $\tilde{Z}_t = \varepsilon_t^z$ and $\tilde{G}_t = 0$ (government consumption). Thus, yielding the expression:

$$\tilde{I}_t = \left[\frac{1-\varsigma(\phi-1)}{\omega_1(1+\lambda_2)}\right]\phi\varepsilon_t^z > 0, \tag{1.9}$$

Where $\tilde{I}_t$ denotes investment, and $0 < \varsigma(\phi-1) < 1$, with $\omega_I = I/Y$: that is, the output shares of investment, thus $\omega_C + \omega_I + \omega_G = 1$. Therefore, the transition paths for the capital stock $\tilde{K}_t$ and consumption $\tilde{C}_t$ we can show as follows:

$$\begin{bmatrix} \tilde{K}_t \\ C_t \end{bmatrix} = \left[\begin{pmatrix} \frac{\delta}{1-\lambda_1} \end{pmatrix}\tilde{I}_t \\ C_t \end{bmatrix}(1-\lambda_1)^{t} \text{ For t = 1, 2, 3 ...} \tag{1.10}$$

Where the term $-\lambda_1$ is < 0, and denotes the stable (negative) characteristic root of Δ_I. Therefore, with respect to the impulse response for transitory shock, technology would return to its steady state level $((\tilde{Z}_t = 0)$ for t = 1, 2...) one period after the shock occurred. This therefore implies that, from equation (1.10), the economy would have a relatively higher capital stock in period one (this is due to $\tilde{K}_1 = \delta \tilde{I}_t > 0$) and subsequently declines over time. Similarly, consumption would also gradually return to its original steady-state value. In terms of investment and employment, they are likely to fall below their respective steady-state levels during transition, especially, given that $(\tilde{I}_t < 0)$ and $(\tilde{L}_t < 0)$ for t = 1, 2 ..., including the real interest rate $\tilde{r}_t < 0$. Under these circumstances, the expectation will be for households to choose a downward sloping consumption status. To complete this analysis, we can now examine the permanent shock scenario as propounded by the RBC models.

Permanent Shock $(\rho z = 1)$

The other form of technology shock is the permanent shock. This type of technology process features a unit root $(\rho z = 1)$. Therefore, the impact on consumption we can express as follows:

$$\tilde{C}_t = \frac{\phi[\lambda_2 - \xi\omega_C]\varepsilon_t^z}{\lambda_2[\omega_C + \phi - 1]} > 0. \tag{1.11}$$

This implies that consumption rises on impact as the permanent technology shock leads to the representative agent wealthier. Equally, the effects for employment, the wage and output are as follows:

$$\tilde{L}_t = \left(\frac{\phi - 1}{\varepsilon_L}\right)\left[1 - \frac{[\lambda_2 - \varsigma\omega_C]}{\lambda_2[\omega_C + \phi - 1]}\right]\varepsilon_t^z, \tag{1.12}$$

$$\tilde{W}_t = \left[\frac{1 - \phi(1 - \varepsilon_L)}{\varepsilon_L}\right]\varepsilon_t^z + \left[\frac{(\phi - 1)(1 - \varepsilon_L)}{\varepsilon_L}\right]\tilde{C}_t > 0, \tag{1.13}$$

$$\tilde{Y}_t = \left[\frac{\lambda_2 - \varsigma(\phi-1)}{\lambda_2[\omega_C + \phi-1]} \right] \phi\omega_C\varepsilon_t^Z > 0. \tag{1.14}$$

Furthermore, we can derive the impact effect on investment from, equation (1.11) and hence, setting $\tilde{Z}_t = \varepsilon_t^z$, and $\tilde{G}_t = 0$, to yield the expression:

$$\tilde{I}_t = \frac{\varsigma\phi\omega_c\varepsilon_t^Z}{\omega_1\lambda_2} > 0 \tag{1.15}$$

Therefore, by setting $(\rho z = 1)$ allows for the analytical expressions for the transition paths of capital stock and consumption, which we can state as:

$$\begin{bmatrix} \tilde{K}_t \\ \tilde{C}_t \end{bmatrix} = \begin{bmatrix} 0 \\ \tilde{C}_t \end{bmatrix} (1-\lambda_1)^t + \begin{bmatrix} \tilde{K}_\infty \\ \tilde{C}_\infty \end{bmatrix} [1 - (1-\lambda_1)^t], \tag{1.16}$$

Where equation (1.11) above gives the definition for $\tilde{C}_t$, thus $\tilde{K}_\infty$ and $\tilde{C}_\infty$ we can define as:

$$\tilde{K}_\infty = \left(\frac{\omega_C}{1-\omega_1} \right) \tilde{C}_\infty = \frac{\phi\omega_C\varepsilon_t^Z}{\omega_G(\phi-1) + \phi\omega_C\varepsilon_L} > 0. \tag{1.17}$$

In addition, $\tilde{K}_t$ and $\tilde{C}_t$ in equation (1.16) we can also define as the weighted average of the relevant impact and long-run effects, with the transition speed of the economy, $(1-\lambda_1)$ determining the time varying weights.

Therefore, for the permanent productivity shock, consumption and the capital stock increase in the long run\\. Thus given the steady state $\tilde{I}_\infty = \tilde{K}_\infty$ and $\tilde{r}_\infty = 0$, meaning that $\tilde{Y}_\infty = \tilde{K}_\infty$, such that $\tilde{K}_\infty - \tilde{L}_\infty = \tilde{W}_\infty = (1/\varepsilon_L)\tilde{Z}_\infty$, where $\tilde{Z}_\infty = \varepsilon_t^Z$. In which case, with constant government spending $\tilde{G}_t = 0$, the steady state for $\tilde{C}_\infty$ and $\tilde{Y}_\infty$ as well as $\tilde{L}_\infty$ can be solved as:

$$\tilde{Y}_\infty = \left(\frac{\omega_C}{\omega_C + \omega_G} \right) \tilde{C}_\infty = \frac{\phi \omega_C \tilde{Z}_\infty}{\omega_G (\phi - 1) + \phi \omega_C \varepsilon_L} > 0. \tag{1.18}$$

$$\tilde{L}_\infty = \frac{\tilde{Y}_\infty - \tilde{C}_\infty}{1 + \omega_{LL}} = -\left(\frac{\omega_G}{\omega_C + \omega_G} \right) \left(\frac{\tilde{C}_\infty}{1 + \omega_{LL}} \right) \leq 0. \tag{1.19}$$

In terms of the long-run effect, a permanent productivity improvement would make a representative agent or firm wealthier, thereby inducing an increase in consumption. Under such circumstances, the investment-capital ratio and the output-capital ratio will remain unaltered but the capital-labour ratio would rise including the real wage. Therefore, given the absence of government consumption, $(\omega_G = 0)$ the income and substitution effects in labor supply will cancel out and employment will remain unchanged. Equally, with positive government consumption, the income effect will dominate the substitution effect and the labor supply declines (in other words, implying more leisure consumption by the household).

Having explained what we mean by cycles, technology shocks and their effects, I can now focus on the predictions of the RBC model and what it intends to achieve.

The RBC model predictions emphasizes on the mechanisms, which involves propagation over time of the effects of shocks. In addition, it focuses on the extent to which shocks that initiate the cycles are real as opposed to monetary in origin. Furthermore, the RBC model has been successful in explaining some of the empirical regularities associated with economic fluctuations (see for example, McCallum (1989) and Plosser (1989)). **The RBC model in addition, emphasises supply or technology disturbances as the main source of macroeconomic fluctuations in a world characterised by rational individuals and perfectly flexible prices.** In other words, in RBC models, productivity disturbances motivate rational agents to adjust savings and investment to smooth consumption and to adjust employment in response to changes in relative price of leisure and the productivity of labor.

One of the merits of the RBC is that its structural equation derivation is from an optimisation (Minford and Sofat (2004)). Thus, the parameters of the model, that is, preferences or technology we can assume as structural. Equally, the model is an equilibrium model and by definition, the construction is to predict how firms with a relatively stable tastes and technology will decide to respond to known economic shocks or changes in economic structure. All these will permit or enable the use of the model to analyze how important macroeconomic variables are likely to respond to shocks and to identify the economic shock.

The early RBC models of Kydland and Prescott (1982), Long and Plosser (1983) and Hansen (1985), were based on closed economy models, hence the assumption of no externalities, taxes, government expenditure or monetary variables. Since then, the traditional RBC models have undergone substantial extensions, especially on the role of government (Mankiw (1989), Christiano and Eichenbaum (1992), McGrattan (1994) and Cooper (1997)). Others include the role of money, (King and Plosser (1984), Cooley and Hansen (1989)). The model has also incorporated distortionary taxes (Braun (1994)) and open economy extensions (Mendoza (1991), and Correia, Rabelo and Naves (1995)).

As for the criticisms of RBC, the original Kydland and Prescott model was set in non-monetary world, (hence the "real") with efficient markets. The model neglected the impact of monetary policy on business cycles, downplayed the role of market inefficiencies and minimized the importance of unemployment. However, subsequent studies have introduced monetary policy, market inefficiencies and unemployment into modifications of the Kydland and Prescott paradigm.

1.2.3   The Background

The RBC theoretical hypothesis is that output movements are behind the productivity shocks, which affect an economy and lead to shifts in its production function. Although these shocks can be both quick and temporary, they can result to persistent movements in output.

The New Keynesian view on the contrary is that cyclical output movements are predominately the result of demand shocks which have a long lasting although temporary effect on output. In essence, booms and recessions are therefore, regarded as periods of excess demand or supply. To generate cycles in output, the disequilibria cannot adjust quickly by movements in wages or prices. In which case, it is the slow market clearing that explains the persistent output movements. The New Keynesian theory in essence is concerned about accounting for why wages and prices move more sluggishly – implying that in the short run, demand shocks will have significant effects on output.

Stabilization policy is often the method the government and/or the central banks, through monetary and fiscal policies, attempt to control the cycles; that is, demand management. The implication is because of the assumption that fluctuations are a consequence of aggregate demand. Therefore, any policy, which cancels out these movements in aggregate demand, will be successful in controlling output.

On the part of RBC model predictions emphasises focuses on the importance of 'real' factors in determining cycles. This is due to the strong perception that markets clear and information is close to perfect. In other words, the source of output fluctuations will come from 'real' factors, which alter an economy's production function. These are predominately technology or productivity shocks[6]. A crucial part for the explanation of business cycles is to account for how a given shock can generate a sustained movement in output. The cycle dynamics also indicates that cycles have duration of at least several quarters or years. The RBC model response is to consider cycles as generated by the combination of two elements – the impulse and propagation. The impulse is the initial productivity or technology shock. This is a sudden and very short run innovation.

The propagation mechanism on the other hand, explains how the shock generates a persistent movement in output. The propagation mechanism is the key to understanding real business cycles (RBC). This is because, without it, there will be no real explanation of the business cycle. A temporary shock would lead to a change in the equilibrium level of output and a shift in the long-run aggregate supply curve. Once the shock disappears or reverses, the economy would return to its original level. This is one of the aims; this chapter is seeking to produce some evidence.

In terms of the propagation mechanism, one approach is to follow the seminal models of Ramsey (1928) and Diamond (1965), which argues that the persistence in output movement results from sustained increase in capital movements following a productivity shock. The propagation mechanism therefore is the consumption smoothing[7]. The other aim in this thesis is not on that line of RBC analysis per se, but on the effects on employment or hours because of technology shocks. To summarise the

---

[6] The nominal factors include price and money shocks. They have no impact on the real economy when information is complete and prices are flexible. In other words, they have no important role in generating cycles. See Chamberlin and Yueh – Macroeconomics, 2006

[7] A positive productivity shock would increase current income, but if households are permanent income consumers, they will rationally attempt to spread this gain over time to maximise their lifetime utility. To achieve this, is to invest some of the present income gain in capital, which will then lead to higher income generation in subsequent periods.

two models, RBC model argues that output fluctuations are the result of productivity shocks. The New Keynesian approach suggests that cycles are the result of price and wage rigidities, which prevent markets from clearing. Once we acknowledge that output can persistently deviate from its equilibrium level (assume this is the trend level of GDP or appropriately the TFP), we then have a basis for explaining cycles or the resultant influence on employment.

1.3.   RBC Model, Technology Shocks and Aggregate Fluctuations

Despite the identified effects of technology shocks, several studies have criticized its role in generating fluctuations, for example, (Summers (1986) and Mankiw (1989)). Some of the criticism is due to the presumption that a technology shock initiates expansions, and therefore, difficult to explain recessions or downturns by resorting to RBC theoretical reasoning. Gali and Rabanal (2004) provided a sceptical perspective to whether RBC predictions links well with technology shocks by suggesting demand factors as the real force behind the strong positive comovement between output and labour input measures. Among those advocating for the RBC model and its important pivotal impact include Kydland and Prescott (1982), and Prescott (1996).

The proponents of the model assume RBC as the equilibrium responses to exogenous variations in technology, given perfect competition and intertemporal optimising agents. This makes the role of nominal friction and monetary policy secondary. Cooley and Prescott (1995), view was that because of the use of calibrated version of the neoclassical growth model augmented with consumption – leisure choice including a stochastic change in total factor productivity (TFP) as the main source accounting for the majority of economic fluctuations. Still on the subject, King and Rebelo (1999) regarded the RBC model as overstated. Taking technological change as the main driving force for cyclical fluctuation has been questioned (Gali and Rabanal (2004), and

Hartley, Hoover and Salyer (1997)). They evaluated the evidence on the empirical effects of exogenous changes in technology on different variables and their success, thus subsequently refuting the model. To complete the picture, we can now look at the Solow residual angle to technology shocks.

1.3.1   The Solow Residual as Proxy to Technology

RBC models are increasingly a dominant platform in macroeconomics. This is primarily through it's emphasises on the importance of quantitative aspects of business cycles and the provision of a more rigorous analysis through dynamic general equilibrium settings or modelling. In addition, it can account for a sizeable fraction of aggregate fluctuations. For example, Prescott (1986) using the Solow residual as a proxy for technology shocks, calibrates a standard RBC model and obtain result where more than 70% of fluctuations in the artificial economy could be explained by shocks of that nature. According to Albergaria de Magalhaes (2005), the problem with this kind of investigation relates to the role of technology shocks in generating fluctuations.

Equally, Jorgenson and Griliches (1967) used industrial electricity consumption as a proxy to capture variable rates of utilization for capital input, and to take into account input measures that would allow for differences in quality and utilization rates. To formulate stylized facts for countries and to explain the main distinctions between artificial and real economies RBC models are useful, for example, Kanczuk and Faria (2000), Val and Ferreira (2001) for Brazil. These models including Kydland and Prescott (1991), used calibration methods but their adequacy is debatable.

However, Albergaria de Magalhaes (2005) questioned the adequacy of Solow residual as a good proxy for technology shocks and argued that it depends on the measure of productivity. Measures that exclude variable rates of factor-utilization tend to be poor proxies for technology shocks. Conversely, measures that include them have statistical properties that are near to the theoretical assumptions usually made in the RBC models. Studies with similar results include Burnside, Eichenbaum and Rebelo (1996) for the US industry and in Baxter and Farr (2001) using dataset on Canadian firms and US. On the positive side for RBC, King and Rebelo (2000) suggested that the findings do not necessarily imply a major weakness for RBC modelling. This is because models with variable factor-utilization as propagation mechanisms tend to amplify shocks with a small magnitude.

1.3.2 Labor – Hoarding, Productivity and True Technology Shocks

In regards to this hypothesis, productivity measures might exhibit a pro-cyclical pattern. This is because during recession, firms aim to maximise their resources, hence they dismiss some workers and reassign some to other roles. The difficulty is, it is not possible to capture these activities through official statistics and once the economy begins to come out of recession, the normal observation is a rise in production without a corresponding rise in input use (hours). This may seem at first as a productivity gain. The fact is firms had this apparent increase in productivity because of labor hoarding. In other words, the observed rise in productivity was spurious. Summers (1986) critique of Prescott (1986) was on this line, while Mankiw (1989) based his own critique on military build up for US over the period 1948 – 85, thereby, characterising it as demand shock. Shea (1999) made use of accident rate to refine the model for technology shock, thus finding effort per hour pro-cyclical and as such a favourable evidence for labor hoarding.

Burnside, Eichenbaum and Rebelo (1993); Burnside and Eichenbaum (996) examine the sensitivity of TFP measures to labor hoarding by using a modified general method of moments (GMM) procedure. The technique involved estimating the fraction of these measures variance that is due to labor hoarding. Burnside and Eichenbaum (1996) analyze the quantitative importance of capacity utilization rates for RBC models. Their results indicated a propagation mechanism in RBC models through time variable utilization rates, and as a result, the implied volatility of productivity shocks is considerably lower than that predicted by standard RBC models. The model assumption is that capacity utilization under this scenario is endogenous, and therefore, gives a rise to a gap between true technology shocks (non-observable) and TFP measures (Observable). Taking into account these observations, Burnside and Eichenbaum in conclusion, argued that RBC models tend to overestimate the fraction of technology shocks variability that is responsible for business cycles.

1.3.3:   The Invariance Properties of Solow's Productivity Residual

Another important aspect of the Solow residual is the invariance properties. To measure the shift or change of the production function, Solow (1957), indicate that one can simply subtract a Divisia index of input growth from output growth. The main assumption of the derivation is the competition and constant returns to scale (CRS hereafter). Under CRS and competition, the Solow residual measures the pure shift of the production function. Solow regard this method as a means to measure the trend in productivity, hence he took the average rate of growth of the Solow residual as the best measure of the average rate of growth of the Hicks-neutral multiplicative component of the production function.

According to Hall (1989), shifts in product demand and factor supplies do not have effect on the residual. Hence, the conclusion that tests of the invariance property in many industries failed, and the cause to be due to increasing returns and market power. The question therefore is whether the estimated productivity measures have the same properties as those postulated in the RBC models. To answer this question, we can review briefly Hall's (1988, 1990) seminal paper on the invariance properties of the Solow residual. In addition to Hall's contribution, which is imperative for industrial organisations, it provided a criticism of RBC models characterization of technology shocks. According to Hall (1988), the invariance property enunciation is that: "Under competition and constant returns to scale, the Solow residual is assumed to be uncorrelated with other variables that causes productivity shifts or caused by productivity shifts".

In addition, there was an assumption for perfect competition to enable firms and/or workers to obtain their marginal products and factor shares until it exhaust output. This assumption made it necessary to determine if there is a correlation between measures of productivity and an instrument set. The instruments employed include military spending, international oil prices and the political party of the President. The objective for using the instruments is to capture variables that have no relationship with productivity. However, Hall's result indicated that the productivity measures used have a correlation with the instrumental variables.

The implication of Hall's result is that productivity may exhibit a procyclical pattern even though the economy's production technology remains relatively the same. BF (1997) among others criticized Hall's choice of instruments. Hartley (1994) argued that the Solow residual may not reliably capture technology shocks by using simulated economies constructed from an adopted Hansen and Sargent (1990) flexible, dynamic linear-quadratic equilibrium macro model. In view that these were simulations, the variability in the series arises only from technology shocks and not market power or labor hoarding. In other words, the Solow residuals reflect a specification error rather than technological change. The reason for this conclusion is the low correlation between controlled technology shocks and the Solow residuals calculated from simulation series.

Evans (1992) using quarterly data tested the exogeneity of the Solow residual for the US over the period 1957 – 83; that is, Granger-causality tests including TFP measures and other macroeconomic variables such as monetary aggregates M1, interest rates, government spending, consumer price index and oil prices. The assumption is that if these macroeconomic variables Granger-cause the Solow residual, then productivity measures is not exogenous. The results showed that TFP measures are Granger-caused by the monetary aggregates used, interest rate and government spending. The other concern relates to the fraction of TFP impulses attributable to demand shocks. On the contrary, Otto (1999), Paquet and Robidoux (2001) using a corrected measure for Canadian economy found these measures are not Granger-caused by any of the macroeconomic variables. This now brings us to the issues of conjectures made by RBC proponents.

Karl Popper (1959, 1972) viewed science as progresses through a series of bold conjectures subjected to severe tests, with some false and accordingly refuted. The truth by definition survives and is unrefuted. Hartley et al (1997) argued that RBC models are bold conjectures in the Popperian mould and refuted based on the preponderance of the evidence. The assessment of the model focused on the original Kydland and Prescott model and its successor models. Despite all the critiques, there are some novelties with the RBC models. We can explore some of them below.

1.3.4 The Novelty of RBC Models

This section reviews the historical development of the real business cycle models. The Solow (1956, 1970) neoclassical growth model is a very good example to start with. For instance, aggregate output (Y) is in the model in accordance to constant returns to scale production function $F(\cdot)$ with aggregate capital K, labor L and a production technology represented by T, hence the production function expression as:

$$Y = F(K,L,T)$$

$$(1.20)$$

The model went on to derive consumption from a Keynesian function as:

$$C = (1-s)Y$$

$$(1.21)$$

Where s is the marginal propensity to save. Therefore, with an assumption to achieve long-term growth, saving (S) is set equal to investment (I) ex ante and ex post:

$$I = S$$

$$(1.22)$$

Capital depreciates at the rate δ and grows with investment I. The following expression represents the relationship:

$$K = I - \delta K = sY - \delta K$$

$$(1.23)$$

where $\dot{K}$ denotes the rate of change of capital while labor grows exogenously at the rate n per unit time, and labor augmenting technology t improves at the rate g per cent per unit time. The effective labor growth at $n + g$ and given the above expressions, the economy will converge to a steady state. Along the steady state growth path, both capital and effective labor will grow at the rate $n + g$. Equally, as the inputs to production are growing at that steady rate, the same will apply to output. Therefore, with the assumption of savings equal to investments, the model will remain in equilibrium but not necessarily in steady state. Hence, whenever the economy moves away from the steady state, for instance, a change in s or n, it will induce changes in capital and output and as a result, adjustments to a new steady state.

In addition, Lucas (1975) adopted the Solow growth model to analyse business cycles. In Lucas (1972, 1973), business cycle was viewed as the reaction of workers and firms to expectation errors induced by monetary policy. Therefore, to shift from short-term expectation errors to long run cycles, Lucas provided a distinction between impulses that begin a business cycle and propagation mechanisms that perpetuate a cycle. The assumption is that expectation errors were the impulses responsible for shifting the economy away from the steady state.

In terms of the after shocks, the economy will remain in disequilibria until there is a correction to the expectation errors. The process of adjusting capital in order to return to steady state is the propagation mechanism. In accordance with the new classical economics of transforming macroeconomic to microeconomic foundations, Lucas replaced the stripped-down demand of the Solow growth model with an assumption of utility-maximizing choices of a representative agent. A representative agent chooses consumption and labour supply by solving a dynamic, intertemporal optimisation problem. However, there is still a fundamental problem with the aggregate demand pathologies. This is because in Lucas's model, the agents use the same savings and investment decisions. In addition, labour supply responded elastically to temporarily high real wages.

Kydland and Prescott (1982) on the other hand, hold a different view from Lucas's model in that there is no monetary sector, while technology shocks or deviation of t in equation (1.20) above from trend provides the impulse to business cycles. Equally, there are no expectation errors in the model. Therefore, technological change has real effects. It is the finding of impulses in technology shocks and the modelling of the economy in continuous equilibrium that distinguishes the real business cycle model from earlier business cycle models. The value of the depreciation rate (δ) is also calibrated in the same appropriate fashion. Similarly, equations (1.21) and (1.22) represent aggregate demand in the Solow growth model and are substitutes in RBC models by an optimisation problem for a representative agent, holding both the consumer and producer roles. The representative agent maximizes a utility function as:

$$U = U (\{C_t\}, \{L_t\}) \tag{1.24}$$

This is subject to current and future production constraints given by equation (1.21) in addition to equation (1.20). In this case, the first set $\{C_t\}$ is the set of current and future levels of consumption, while $\{L_t\}$ is the set for current and future supplies of labor. The calibrated model is non-linear and to solve the model, the equation requires reformulation as linear approximations around the unknown steady state. From this point, RBC models abstract from the concerns of traditional growth theory, without seeking any explanation for the steady state but instead concentrated on (equilibrium) deviations from the steady state. Therefore, transforming the Cobb-Douglas production function (1.20) will give

$$\text{Log } (Z) = \log(Y) - \theta\log (L) - (1 - \theta) \log (K), \tag{1.25}$$

That is, the empirical measure of the technology parameter usually, referred to as the Solow residual. Estimating this using actual data will show a trend. Furthermore, it will imply $g \neq 0$, therefore needs detrending before being use as input to the real business cycle model. Detrended log (Z) is the state-variable T, or technology shock. Generally, t will be a persistent process; for example, $T_t = \rho T_{t-1} + \varepsilon_t$ with $\rho > 0$ and ε_t an independent, identically distributed random variable. As we shall see in subsequent chapters of this book, the data used in estimating contractionary effects undergo the HP filtering and detrending including, stationary test and heterogeneity test. I will explain about HP filter later in this chapter. So what are the views from the tests? The next subsection sheds some lights to this question.

1.3.5 Perceptions on Testing

This chapter has so far discussed to some extent the RBC model and as such, it is necessary to ascertain what exactly the RBC model is supposed to explain and then test them accordingly. Real Business Cycle model has traditionally attempted to predict what causes output to fall and then rise again. Therefore, when output declines, the expectation is for employment, income and trade to decline accordingly.

Equally, when technology improves, the RBC prediction is that employment will rise. The RBC theorists believe technology is the driving force behind the business cycle.

The structural vector autoregressive model (SVAR) is increasingly becoming the estimation of the most preferred platform that are currently being employed in analysing the role of technological change as a source of permanent fluctuations in labour productivity to identifying technology shocks. An example is the Canova et al (1994) examination of the implications of calibrated RBC model for the dynamic behaviour of various time series. Eichenbaum (1991) provided analysis on the issue of parameter choice by observing that the numerical values of the underlying parameters used to calibrate a real business cycle model are indeed estimates of the true values. The fact is that, true values like depreciation rate or the variance of the shock to the Solow residual are unknown. The problem is because the estimated numbers came from sample data, of which there are associated sampling errors. See also Farmer (1993) comparison between RBC model and one with different principles of construction, based on an economy with increasing returns to scale and shocks. The attempted to capture the dynamics of the economy by using vector autoregression model for the actual economy and the application of the estimated equations to generate the path the economy would follow.

1.3.6   The Impulse Mechanism

A prominent distinguishing feature of the RBC model centres on its ability to locate the impulse to business cycles in technology shocks. The overarching question then is what evidence exists that technology shocks are the principal impulse driving the business cycle? The formal answer to the question is, technology shocks are the deviations of the parameter *t* in the aggregate production function, from its steady-state growth path. By averaging, it should reduce the variability of the aggregate shocks relative to the underlying shocks to individual technology level, including changes in the legal and regulatory system within a country[8]. Solow (1957) explicitly observed that idle capacity biases the measure and that the measure hinges on the assumption of factors receiving their marginal products. To enable us to explore in more detail the impulse mechanism behind aggregate productivity and aggregate technology, we have to review further the RBC theory.

1.3.7   The Propagation Mechanism

The idea behind the propagation mechanism contained in RBC model predictions is that it should transmit and amplify the impulses to the various cyclical aggregates. In that sense, combining with the shocks it should provide explanation for the pattern of fluctuations in each series and for their comovements. Take for example, Watson (1993) adoption of a spectral analysis to decompose the power of the real business cycle model to match movements in output at different frequencies. The finding was that the spectral power of RBC model is high at low frequencies (2 – 8 years). Cogley and Nason (1995b) therefore, compared the dynamic pattern of the technology shocks fed into the RBC model with the predicted time-series for output generated by the

---

[8] Proponents of RBC models have broadened the scope of technology to include 'changes in the legal and regulatory system within a country' (Hansen and Prescott, 1993, p.281).

model. The study found the dynamic properties of the exogenous inputs responsible for determining the properties of the output and not the RBC model itself.

However, Hartley (1997) argued that one of the reasons RBC models seem to do well is due to the reliance on standards of assessment that are not particularly discriminating, especially in its practice of data handling. RBC models predict values for output, consumption, investment and other time series expressed as deviations from the steady state (as discussed above). Therefore, in order to compare these with actual data requires elimination of an estimate of the steady state from these variables, which are trending. The Solow growth model on the other hand suggests that all these variables should grow at rates related to the steady state growth rate. The problem is they are not observable (bearing in mind that RBC models are mainly calibrated simulations). Thus, RBC models follow one of two strategies to generate detrended data: to remove constant exponential trend, which is linear in the logarithm and as such linear detrending, (King et al. (1988)). This is accurate if the rate of growth of the labour force (n) and of technology (ζ) were constant over time.

An alternative strategy is to use a varying trend that effectively allows the steady state growth rate to be variable, and is the option usually implemented using the Hodrick – Prescott (HP) filter, Anyalezu, (2014), Hodrick and Prescott (1997). The HP filter definition assume, $x_t = \bar{x}_t + \hat{x}_t$ where $\bar{x}_t$ represents the trend component and where $\hat{x}_t$ denotes the deviation from trend. The HP filter chooses this decomposition to solve the following problem:

$$\min\left\{(1/T)\sum_{t=1}^{T}\hat{\chi}_t^2 + (\lambda/T)\sum_{t=2}^{T-1}[(\bar{\chi}_{t+1} - \bar{\chi}_t) - (\bar{\chi}_t - \bar{\chi}_t - 1)]^2\right\} \qquad \lambda > 0 \quad (1.26)$$

Where T is the number of observation and λ is a parameter that controls the amount of smoothness in the series. Therefore, if $\lambda = 0$, the smooth series is identical to the original series and if $\lambda = \infty$, it is a linear trend. The optimal value of λ is $\lambda = \sigma_x^2 / \sigma_c^2$ where σ_x and σ_c are the standard deviation of the innovations in trend and in the cycle[9].

In which case, the HP filter is arguably successful in providing a theoretical estimate of the steady state growth path. Cogley and Nason (1995a) showed that pre- filtered data do not generate cycles in a real business cycle model, while HP-filtered data does. In addition, when the input data serially correlates, HP filter not only generates spurious cycles but also strongly increases the correlation among the predicted values of output, consumption, investment, hours of work and other values from the RBC model. To use HP filter, is to choose λ a priori to isolate cyclical fluctuations belonging to specific frequency band. In addition, Nelson and Plosser (1982) estimated λ to be in the range of $\left[\frac{1}{6},1\right]$ for most of the series they examine. This means that the variability HP filter attributes to the cyclical component is actually part of the trend. The next section therefore, considers a neutral or agnostic approach.

1.3.8   Neutrality to logarithm level or first difference approach

Given the different views in the literatures about whether technology shocks drive hours up or down, an alternative approach is to adopt a neutral stance. According to some literatures, estimation in levels or in first differences provide opposite conclusions. The reliance on an agnostic procedure meant that there is no choice between specification in log level or in first difference. The finding in Pesavento and Rossi (2004) is that a positive productivity shock has a negative impact effect on hours as in Francis and Ramey (2001), but the effect is much more short-lived and when it becomes positive as in Christiano et al (2003), it is not significant. Some recent literature has questioned the validity of this theoretical implication. For example, Gali (1999) identifies technology

---

[9] See Canova, Fabio (1998) for complete analysis on "Detrending and business cycle facts", Journal of Monetary Economics 41 (1998) 475 – 512.

shocks as the only shocks that have an effect on labor productivity in the long run and therefore, estimate a persistent decline of hours in response to a positive technology shock. In addition, other studies that agree or are of similar findings with these conclusions include Shea (1999), Francis and Ramey (2001). The other general equilibrium models that can account for these empirical findings include, Uhlig (2003), Gali and Rabanal (2004), Basu and Fernald (2004).

On the opposing side, Christiano, Eichenbaum and Vigfusson (2003) disagree with these empirical results. They adopted Gali (1999) identifying assumption and found evidence that a positive technology shock drives hours worked up, not down. The estimated effects of technology shocks essentially depend on whether the empirical analysis is a specification of hours and technology in levels or in differences. The studies by Gali, Shea, Francis and Ramey were specifications in first differences with report that hours worked fall after a positive technology shock. The CEV (2003) study used hours in levels and reported that hours worked rose; hence the postulation that, "The difference must be due to different maintained assumptions". In nutshell, what this means is that, it depends on the treatment of hours worked.

Pesavento and Rossi (2004), argument that whether hours worked is a stationary or exactly integrated process is a key assumption in the current debate on the effects of technology shocks in business cycles. It is difficult to decide between specifications in levels and in first difference solely based on unit root tests. The reason is unit root tests have low power. Equally, impulse responses based on VARs estimated in levels or in first differences have adverse coverage properties as well. This is of course, unless the true data generating process is not persistent; in which case, levels are appropriate. If it has an exact unit root, then first differences are appropriate.

The neutrality (or agnostic) approach as is in Pesavento and Rossi (2003) does not impose a unit root or stationarity test. Similarly, with robustness to the presence of highly persistent processes, it is therefore appropriate for analysing the long run effect of technology shocks on hours worked without making assumptions about integration of the series. It is this reached conclusion that prompted the claims of a positive productivity shock with a negative impact effect on hours worked, even though it does disappears quickly (after only 2 quarters), and then becomes positive as in CEV (2003) but not significantly different from zero. In the CEV framework, the level specification implies that the first difference specification is a mis-specification, while the first difference specification indicates that the level specification is correct. The different specification came from the fact that the level VAR allows for a unit root. The impact of these biases depends on the economic problem at hand and on the particular parameters in consideration. Therefore, neglecting the effect may lead to a very different economic outcome in measuring the effects of productivity shocks.

In table 1.0, I provide a summary of research literatures that have investigated the effects of technology shocks and aggregate fluctuations. The listings in the table provided a contrast on findings between those for and against contractionary effects on hours or employment after a positive technology shocks. In the table, I start by examining some of the empirical studies with similar findings as Gali (1999), followed by those with opposite results. The summary also contains the methodological approach (further details are also provided in the footnote) and a brief explanation of their findings.

Table 1.0 Summaries of Literatures Reviewed: Technology Shocks & aggregate Fluctuations

Paper	Method & Data Source	For / Against Contraction	Explanation
Anyalezu (2011)	Panel data & SVAR Annual data, BEID, ONSLFS, OECD, OPEC, WDS-IEA, SPIRI & Jenkins Defence	For	Two identifying techniques used to model the effects on employment following a technological innovation at the aggregate level. Evidence from the study shows hours worked fall or rise after a positive permanent technology shock, depending on the empirical treatment of hours. The correlation between technology and hours indicates strong positive co-movements. Productivity shows positive co-movement with hours.
Gali & Rabanal (2004)	VAR Quarterly US data: Haver USECON database	For	The study questions reliance of changes in aggregate technology as a key factor behind business cycles, in contrast to RBC models claim. They argue that demand factors are the main driver for the strong positive co-movement between output and labor input measures, which characterises RBC models.
Gali (1999 & 2004)	Structural VAR US quarterly data: Citi base, and by construction, OECD Quarterly National Accounts (G7)	For	The study identifies technology shocks as the only shock with permanent effects on labor productivity in the long run. The study estimated a persistent decline of hours in response to positive technology shocks.

Blanchard, Solow & Wilson (1995)	Instrumental Variable, Approach with demand side[10].	For	A regression of changes in unemployment on the filtered productivity growth variable gave a positive coefficient. This means that an increase in productivity drives the unemployment rate upwards while; its dynamic specification sees the effect falling to its original level after three quarters.
Gali (2005)	VAR. Data 1948:Q1 – 2003:Q4, OECD & USECON	For	A negative co-movement between hours and consumption, except for Japan. Technology shock shows major discrepancies with the predictions of standard RBC models.
BFK (1997 & 2004) BF (2002)	Growth Accounting Methodology[11] Data: Jorgenson dataset, BLS, Haver Analytics	For	Response of estimation to improvements in their measure of technological change indicates a decline on impact for inputs, including labour while output shows no significant change. Post the short run impact, both variables rises with labour input returning to its original level and output attaining a higher level several years after the shock.

---

[10] The variables are assumed to be orthogonal to exogenous technological change used as instruments for employment growth. Alternatively, it can be assumed as change in unemployment in a regression featuring productivity growth as a dependent variable. The fitted residual is then interpreted as a proxy for technology driven changes in productivity.

[11] The method allowed for various estimations to be done which includes: increasing returns, imperfect competition, variable factor utilization and sectoral compositional effects. The Purified technology in the model can be assumed as an effort to correct the measurement error in Solow (1957) residual due to assumptions fundamental in its derivation.

Shea (1998)	A DGE Method[12]. Examines time series interactions between measures of technology change e.g. R & D and economic activity. Data from NBER (annual)	Against	Innovation in technology shows no significant change in TFP; however it increases labour inputs in the short run. The VAR specification with a significant increase in TFP in response to positive technology shocks shows inputs moving in opposite direction to TFP.
Blanchard & Quah (1989)	Dynamic Effects VAR model using quarterly US data 1950:2 – 1987:4. Data from BLS. Aggregate	For	In accordance with traditional Keynesian model, the view was that increases in productivity could lead to increase in unemployment in the short run. This is if aggregate demand fails to rise sufficiently to sustain employment[13].
Blanchard (1989)	SVAR Data: (not disclosed in the paper)	Against	A dynamic effect showing a rise in unemployment. The model uses direct restrictions on the contemporaneous SR effects of innovations on the X variable.
Kiley (1997)	Structural VAR[14].	For	The result indicate technology generate a negative correlation between employment and output growth.

---

[12] The modelling is used to provide a link between changes in measures of technological innovation and subsequent changes in TFP and hired inputs using industry level data.

[13] The model identifies 2 types of disturbances generating unemployment and output dynamics – permanent and transitory effects (as supply and demand). The demand effect has no LR effect on unemployment or output. The supply disturbances have no effect on unemployment, but may have LR effect on output.

[14] The SVAR model was an extension of Gali (1999) to data from two-digit manufacturing industries.

Khan & Tsoukalas (2006)	VAR Model Data: Ellen McGrattan and Valerie Ramey datasets, quarterly data & from Groth et al (2005)	For	Reported the response of labour input to neutral and investment specific technology shocks in the UK data. The result shows that hours worked decline, which they attribute to the large negative correlation between labour productivity and hours.
Franco & Philippon (2006)	Structural VAR[15]. Aggregate. Synthetic data, Jorgenson & Stiroh sectoral dataset (2000).	For	The model is to examine the role of permanent and transitory shocks for firms and aggregate dynamics. The findings show that technology shocks induce a negative comovement between output and hours, and uncorrelated across industries.
Francis, Owyang & Theodorou (2003)	A bivariate VAR with labor productivity and labor hours.[16] Data: BLS (1948:Q1 – 2000:Q4) time series.	For	The result indicates a negative response of hours to a positive technology shock. The model also assumes technology is the only shock with a long-horizon impact on labor productivity, irrespective of VAR estimated with labour hours in levels or in first differences. The model also used an agnostic algorithm proposed by Uhlig (1999) to implement a long run (LR) restriction.

---

[15] The estimated SVAR has three shocks – (1) technology with permanent effects on industry productivity; (2) composition shocks with permanent effects on the industry share in total output and (3) transitory shocks.

[16] This is a variant of the sign restriction algorithm of Uhlig (1999).

Francis & Ramey (2003a)	Structural VAR[17]	For	Both the augmented model with capital tax rates and the model with alternative identifying restrictions indicate similar impulse responses to technology shocks as in Gali (1999). Hours declined in response to a positive technology shock.
Francis & Ramey (2003b)	Structural VAR with long run identifying restrictions.	For	Using long-term UK annual time series, they show evidence of a negative short run impact of technology shocks on labor.
Francis & Ramey (2004)	VAR Data: annual data from BLS, US Census, mini historical stats table HS-3, Econ report of the President 2003 table B-34, Digest of Educ. Stats 2002 H-442, Claudia Goldin – NBER WP H0119	For	The study modifies standard adjustments to generate hour's per capita series that corresponds with theoretical model. The effects of technology on hours are negative.

---

[17] The model provided an extension to Gali (1999). Their modification include augmenting the baseline VAR with specification in first differences using a capital tax rate as proxy for the impact of technology shocks from those of permanent changes in tax rates. In addition, technology shocks were identified as those with permanent effects on real wages in contrast to labour productivity or hours. The alternative identification restrictions were not rejected when added to a unified (over-identified) model.

Carlsson (2000)	This is a variant of BFK (1999) and Burnside et al (1995). Data: Annual aggregate	For	The study created a time series for technological change. The application was for Swedish two digit manufacturing industries. Positive technology shocks show a contractionary effect on hours and a non-expansionary impact on output.
Marchetti & Nucci (2005)	A dynamic cost minimization model with adjustment costs, a variant of BK (1997)[18]. Data[19]: SIM & CADS for the period 1984 – 1997.	For	Used firm level estimates of technology change to assess the impact on labor input growth. The result shows that positive technology improvements tend to decline labor input on impact. The conclusion was that, the finding is coherent with the prediction of a sticky price model. Thus, provides evidence of a connection at the firm level between the degree of price rigidity and the intensity of the contractionary effect of technology shocks.
Alexius & Carlsson (2005)	SVAR Data: Quarterly & annual - NIPA BEA, Dale Jorgenson database, SNEPQ dataset, OECD MEI, IFS, Mark W. Watson dataset, BLS. Aggregate – U.S & Swedish	For	They estimated technology change from 2 versions of production function approach and 2 SVAR models. Technology improvements are associated with contemporary contractions in input and hours with no significant increase in output.

---

[18] The model uses Basu and Kimball (1997) proposed methodology to derive a measure of technology change and estimate the model on firm level panel data for a representative sample of Italian manufacturing firms.

[19] Data sources: SIM = The Bank of Italy's survey of investment in manufacturing; CADS = the company accounts data service reports.

CEV (2003) (2004)	VAR[20] Data: used the aggregate technology series computed in BFK (1999)[21]	Against	Their result show that hours worked rise after a positive shock to technology. The same identification procedure as in Gali (1999), was used, with hours specified in log level.
CEV (2003)	VAR: for US & Canada. Data: see footnote[22]	Against	The model examines the response of hours worked to a permanent technology shock. With annual data from Canada, hours worked rise after a positive technology shock. It is same result using annual data from the U.S. It contradicts models claiming positive technology shock causes hours worked to fall. They attribute the different results to the models making a specification error in the statistical model or per capita hours worked. They also show that Canadian monetary policy accounted for technology shocks.
Vigfusson (2004)	VAR Data: from the BLS KLEMS dataset, IMF world price of oil	Against	In response to a positive technology shock, a standard flexible price model would have an immediate increase in hours worked. The response by per capita hours worked to a technology shock is initially small but later increases.

---

[20] Using the aggregate technology series computed in BFK (1999), they show the impact on hours worked after a positive shock to technology.

[21] CEV (2003) result based on quarterly US time series data.

[22] The U.S data used is the annual version of the data used in CEV (2003). Due to short span of Canadian quarterly data, they used annual data instead from 1961 (CANSIM).

Mikhail (2005)	BVAR Data: DRI Economics database Quarterly data 1948:1 –2000:3	Against	This examines the effect of a positive technology shock on per capita hours worked within the class of Bayesian Vector Auto-Regressive (BVAR) models. This was to avoid debate whether specification of per capita hours is in levels or first difference stationary. In addition, it considered six priors after technology shock. The marginal posteriors of the VAR parameters were generatedz using the Markov Chain Monte Carlo (MCMC) Gibbs sampler, yielding similar results from the VAR. Using CEV data and imposing the identifying restriction, the results indicate per capita hours rise following a positive technology.
Burnside & Eichenbaum (1996)	A GMM dynamic aggregate model - a variant of Hansen (1985) model[23]. Data: US Dept of Commerce (1994), NIPA, BGFRS[24], Citibase for period 1955:Q1 – 1992: Q4.	Against	The model estimated an equilibrium RBC model where capital utilization varies over the business cycle, and is an important source of propagation to business cycle shocks. The result shows hours worked increased follow an impact.

---

[23] The model is modified to accommodate factor hoarding expressed as variable capital utilization rates and varying labour effort. It incorporates a different approach to estimating time varying capital utilisation. The distinction between the model measure of hours worked and that of Hansen is that, relate to their low frequency behaviour. Hansen series has a larger degree of high frequency variation.

[24] BGFRS = the Board of Governors of the Federal Reserve System.

Shapiro (1993)	Instrumental Variable. Aggregate, annual & quarterly: Bureau of the Census (Survey of plant capacity), Wayne B. Gray TFP dataset	Against	Empirical studies of productivity finds short run increasing returns to labor. Taking capital & hours into account, there appear to be no short run increasing returns to conventionally measured total factor inputs.
Altig, Christiano, Eichenbaum & Linde (2002) & (2004)	VAR from estimated equilibrium model (simulation). Data: DRI Basic Economics database, quarterly 1959:Q1-2001:Q4. DGEM b/4 aggregate	Against	Their (2002) paper indicates that positive technology shock drives hours worked up. In the (2004) paper, they constructed a DGEM of cyclical fluctuations. Result shows low correlation between inflation, marginal cost and other inflation inertia. It favors the firm specific capital specification due to micro implications.
Alves, Brandao de Brito, Gomes & Souza (2006)	SVAR Data: Eurostat, ECB, EC, OECD, Fagan et al. ((2001) hereafter AWM database)[25] 1970:1 – 2004:Q3	Against	Evidence shows hours raise following technology shocks. The result also supports hours as stationary in levels.
Shapiro & Watson (1988)	A Neoclassical Growth regression & Instrumental Variables; Quarterly US data 1951: - 1987:2, from BLS	Against	The level of output is determined in the LR by supply shocks like technology and labor supply. Positive technology shocks provide evidence for strong growth. No restrictions imposed on SR & LR, but on real interest rate; hence labor was allowed to have a stochastic trend.

---

[25] AWM = Area-Wide Model database, EC = European Commission.

Yi Wen (1999)	VAR (a modified Kydland & Prescott model) Data: Citibase	Against	RBC comoves with output. Technology shock reducing consumption and commove with output.
Pesavento & Rossi (2004)	VAR Data from Christiano et al, DRI Economics database, quarterly: 1948:Q1 – 2001:Q4	Against	Depending on the estimation in levels or in first difference. The reliance in estimating the model is one of "agnostic" procedure[26]. Hence, a positive productivity shock has a negative impact on hours and then becomes positive at business cycle frequencies[27].
Faust & Leeper (1997)	Bayesian Monte Carlo Procedure in RATS (VAR) Data: (Simulation) considered both quarterly and annual data frequencies.		This investigates the reliance of imposing restrictions on the long run effects of shocks in VAR models. Argued that LR identifying scheme is weak and structural inference by the VAR must satisfy strong dynamic restrictions. Hence, requires care to assess the robustness of inference.
Chang and Hong (2006) & (2003)	VAR of 458 4-Digit US manufacturing industries 1958 – 1996. Data: from NBER (annual) Manufacturing Productivity Database	Against	Their result shows that technological improvement increases employment in many US manufacturing industries. The result differs from those based on labor productivity that found a negative correlation between the permanent component

---

[26] This implies a sort of 'atheist', that is the research does not have to choose whether to do the specification in log levels or in first differences.

[27] The result shows negative effect on hours as in Francis and Ramey (2001), but the effect is much shorter lived than previously found as it disappears after only two quarters. When it becomes positive, it is as in Christiano et al. (2003) but not significantly different from zero.

			of labour productivity and employment in manufacturing. Their view was that TFP is the best measure for technology because labour productivity reflects the input mix as well as technology.

In table 1.2 below, I show the number of review literatures that are for contraction and the number against in their respective studies. The table also contain the number of studies that used quarterly data, the number that used annual data and the number that used both. In this research, both forms of data were used. The data uses are appropriately explained in all the chapters accordingly.

Table 1.2: Summaries of Reviewed Papers: Technology Shocks & Aggregate Fluctuations

	For Contraction	No paper Against	Qtr & Annual	Qtr	Annual
No of paper Agg Data Qtr	8	8	3	15	19
No paper non aggregate	10	9			

Having established the above definitions of TFP and RBC theories, it is also essential to review the economic growth theories of the neoclassical and endogenous growth models. The models are relevant in estimating TFP and as such will form the discussion in the next section.

1.4   Conclusions

We have presented here a major aim of this chapter, which is to provide a comprehensive literature survey covering TFP and RBC models. Through this process, there is a perception of an acceptance that TFP is important. This is more so given that increasing productivity relates to increased economic growth, lower costs and sustained competitiveness. For example, the most widely used productivity indicators for firms are labour productivity – units of output, or value added, per employee. Nevertheless, these measures have drawbacks. The most important one being the failure to account for the reason labour productivity increased in accordance with RBC models predictions.

A possible solution therefore, lies in the Solow residual measurement, TFP. This is because using Solow's approach and the concept of TFP as a microeconomic tool can facilitate analysis and separation of labour productivity change in individual firms. In terms of aggregate level, Kuznet's (1971 p.73) international comparisons attributed economic growth to the Solow (1957) residual (TFP). Productivity growth is exogenous within the simplest version of Solow's model. Both Kuznet (1971) and Solow (1957) regard productivity to predominate among the sources of economic growth hence, most of growth is exogenously determined. In which case, reliance on the Solow residual as an explanatory factor is a powerful indictment of the limitations of the neoclassical framework (see Dougherty and Jorgenson (2003)).

Furthermore, standard neoclassical growth theory has not provided a suitable explanation for the immense inequality in the wealth of nations. Most theories of TFP, for example, Parente and Prescott (1999), ignored the potential role of barriers to capital accumulation in generating aggregate TFP differences (Diego Restuccia, (2002), (especially across countries or firms)). Without doubt, there has been an upsurge of interest in the measurement and explanation of TFP and RBC models because of the development of new theoretical models, the availability of new and better data and estimation techniques. The advent of advancement of econometrics has made possible the testing of refined hypotheses. Nonetheless, the issues involved are too numerous and too complex, and the available empirical evidence too diverse to allow bold conclusions about the measurement and the determinants of TFP and RBC models in aggregate fluctuations.

1.6   The Aims and Scope of the Study

The research for this book focuses on the empirical estimation of Total Factor Productivity (TFP) and Contractionary Effects for the UK for the period 1970 – 2000. The aim is to test the hypothesis on the impact of technology on productivity and employment or hours worked following a positive technology shocks. The study therefore, using UK economy data examines the UK private business economy. The purpose is to investigate the aggregate manufacturing sector of the economy and then disaggregate into manufacturing and non-manufacturing sectors, durable and non-durable sectors. The other objective of this book is to investigate the predictions of the Real Business Cycle Models in relation to the impact on productivity and employment / hours worked through a bivariate vector autoregressive model (BSVAR) and a 5 variable VAR model (high dimension). This will then enable the study to look for evidence of contractionary effects in the UK private business economy.

Therefore, the scope of the research will be limited to:

1) The estimation of total factor productivity (TFP) or the Solow residual (SR).
2) The estimation for aggregate fluctuations and technology shocks.
3) Given the established scenarios, the estimation at disaggregate and aggregate levels using labour productivity and TFP growth shocks to examine the relationship between hours (employment) and productivity though a bivariate structural autoregressive model (BSVAR). This provides a means for checking contractionary effect evidence in the UK private economy.

1.7 The Book Organisation

I provide herewith a snapshot or an overall scheme of the book. In other to achieve the aims of the studies stated above, there are 5substantive chapters presented in the book. This introductory and literature review is chapter one. It discussed and provided the literature review that relates to the research. Chapter one importantly provided some insights into the underlying refined methodologies for modelling TFP in conjunction with the real business cycle models. The chapter fundamentally discusses the competing approaches to estimating contractionary effects using structural vector autoregressive models (SVARs), at industry firm-level and aggregate level.

The empirical estimation of TFP forms the next substantive chapter (2) of this thesis. The chapter establish the mechanics or the empirical econometrics procedures for the estimation of aggregate productivity and aggregate technology for the whole UK including the manufacturing sector. Chapter 3 provide details of the estimation of TFP using a modified Solow Residual or Purified Technology that is, including hours. This modification embedded in the estimation makes chapter 3 to be distinct from chapter 2. The aim in chapter 3 is to establish if there is any contraction following technology improvement. Chapters 4 and 5 are based on SVARs model. I investigated the issue of contractionary effects by adopting three different methodological approaches namely; Gali (1999) model; Christiano, Eichenbaum and Vigfusson (CEV (2003)) model using BFK measure approach; Chang and Hong (CH (2006)) model. The reason for using the combination of the three different approaches is because of the lack of consensus in the literatures. Some of the findings contradict the predictions of the RBC models. Equally, a few of the model's approach adopted were sceptical of RBC model and as such are critical of its predictions, while others are in favour.

Notes & Discussions

Notes & Discussions

Chapter 2

The Estimation of Aggregate Productivity and Aggregate Technology

2.0   Introduction

This chapter is primarily about the estimation of aggregate productivity and aggregate technology that is, TFP estimation for the UK 1970 – 2000. The empirical modelling will assist to answer some of the research questions discussed in chapter 1. Further more, the TFP empirical modelling in this chapter is confine to the UK aggregate level. The estimations for disaggregated sectors will be in chapter 3. The additional purpose for this chapter is to establish the empirical and theoretical background for the estimation of TFP. The model in this chapter will be more complicated than our illustrative model in chapter 1. However, the principles established in that model is still be applicable to the one developed here.

The following is an outline structure of this chapter. Section 2.1, is the model specification. Section 2.2 is a discussion on the aggregation specification while section 2.3 deals with the implications of the markups. In section 2.4, I describe the data analysis. The empirical result forms the discussion in section 2.5 with conclusions in section 2.6.

2.1   The Model Specification

The first task in this model is to specify the estimation at firm level, after which the aggregate level specification. To do this, I adopted the model proposed by Basu and Fernald (BF (1997, 2002)) and Basu, Fernald and Kimball (BFK (2004)). The motivation for the model procedure is to measure directly technology in comparison with the above-mentioned studies. Secondly, is to show aggregate productivity and aggregate technology can differ due to technological improvement by using UK time series data (annual data). In addition, to see if a strong positive comovement between aggregate productivity and aggregate technology exists and if there is any difference between the two. Therefore, we can commence the empirical modelling by specifying first the firm level value added and productivity. In the model, firms possess a production function for gross output of the form:

$$Y_i = F^i\left(K_i, L_i, M_i, T_i\right) \tag{2.1}$$

Where Y_i is the gross output, the term F^i denoting the firm production function, while the inputs are represented by: K_i for capital, L_i is labor, and M_i for materials. The unobserved input is T_i that is technology, which is homogenous of arbitrary degree γ_i in inputs[28]. Equally, there is no restriction to one of γ_i and as such there may be no constant returns to scale (RTS) in F^i (see Rotemberg and Woodford (1995)). Furthermore, the RTS γ_i is equal to the sum of the output elasticities with respect to all inputs.

In the model, the labor compensation is a proxy for labor for each industry. As illustrated in chapter 1 with our basic model, we can assume that for any input i, the marginal product is F^i_j. Thus, as in BF (2002), the model's first-order condition for firm i indicates that

---

[28] In this equation, the inputs are K_i, L_i, M_i and T_i. Only technology T_i is an unobserved input.

the marginal product is proportional to the shadow rental cost for the input P_{ji} as:

$$P_i F_j^i = \mu_i P_{ji}.$$ (2.2)

Given the absence of observed prices, to be able to estimate the model, prices were derived from capital and value added (total output). Therefore, equation (2.2) in this case shows the relationship between output, factor shares and the markups. The term μ_i defines the mark-up firms can charge above the marginal cost. I therefore have the representation as $\mu_i = P_i / MC_i$ where MC_i is the marginal cost and P_i as the price.

The other reason in addition to the above is due to the research question about imperfect competition. Further more, firms with increasing returns will have to charge markups in order to cover their costs. Where the return to scale (RTS) across firms are different because of technological reasons, for example differences in fixed costs, it follows that the markups charged will be different.

In BF (1997 and 2002), they used Hall (1988) methodology, which is in itself an adoption from Solow (1957) to provide a model for estimating a constant marginal cost mark-up. Therefore, by following Hall (1990) cost minimization approach it implies profit-maximization is not necessary for our derivation. This is because it is a sufficient condition to any form of price-setting behavior. The justification is because it can allow for sticky output prices and for complex dynamic pricing strategies. We shall discuss the issue of sticky prices later in chapter 3 and 4. See also for example, BF (1995), Rotemberg and Saloner (1986) for further explanations. The other reason is that mark-ups do not need to depend on the elasticity of demand as opposed to the neoclassical and endogenous growth models. In this model, the cost minimization approach means that output growth, Δy_i will be equal to the mark-up multiplied by revenue share weighted input growth, Δx_i plus the gross output augmenting technology (Δt_i)[29].

Therefore, by combining the input shares and aggregate technology with equation (2.2) above, where Δi is the input's growth rate, gross output would be:

$$\Delta y_i = \mu_i \left[s_{Li}\Delta l_i + s_{Ki}\Delta k_i + s_{Mi}\Delta m_i \right] + \Delta t_i \equiv \mu_i \Delta x_i + \Delta t_i \qquad (2.3)^{30}$$

The revenue shares would sum to one thereby making it to correspond with the Solow shares. This is the elasticities in the square brackets. If on the other hand, there are economic profits or losses, these shares may not sum to one. Where that applies, it will make it different from the Solow shares. However, the procedure in this model is consistent with a first-order log-linearization of the production function. In my mark-up estimation, I used a pooled instrumental variable, 2SLS fixed effects (cross-sections 34) model. The model sample (adjusted) is from 1970 – 2000. The model included 31 observations after adjustments, with a total pool (balanced) observation of 1054. The instruments used are oil, defence, political and monetary policy shocks[31]. I will discuss on the variables used later. For another form of markup estimation, see Banerjee and Russell (BR (2004)).

In this model, there is a link between the gross output for growth in primary inputs[32], Δx_i^V intermediate inputs, Δm_i and technology shocks. I will explore the effects of technology shocks in more detail

---

[29] Δt_i is expressed in BF (2002) as $\frac{F_T^i}{F^i}\Delta t_i$

[30] Note: $F_T^i T_i / F^i = 1 - \mu_i s_{mi}$ That is, one less the mark-up times the intermediate input share. Therefore, $\Delta t_i = (1 - \mu_i s_{mi})\Delta t_i$ Equation (2.3) is applicable at an instant in time, while the elasticity's and mark-up μ_i may vary overtime.

[31] Note that the estimated average industry markup is μ_i and the share of materials in firm $\bar{\imath}$ is s_{mi}.

[32] See appendix A2.4.

over the next subsequent chapters. In the meantime, the firm level value added, Δv_i specification is:

$$\Delta v_i = \frac{\Delta y_i - s_{Mi}\Delta m_i}{1 - s_{Mi}}$$

$$\Delta y_i - \left[\frac{s_{Mi}}{1 - s_{Mi}}\right](\Delta m_i - \Delta y_i)\,^{33} \tag{2.4}$$

Therefore, by subtracting $\mu_i s_{Mi}\Delta y_i$ from the two sides, and dividing through by $(1 - \mu_i s_{MI})$, gives the output growth as:

$$\Delta y_i = \left[\frac{\mu_i(1 - s_{Mi})}{1 - \mu_i s_{Mi}}\right]\Delta x_i^V + \left[\frac{\mu_i s_{Mi}}{1 - \mu_i s_{Mi}}\right](\Delta m_i - \Delta y_i) + \Delta t_i \frac{\Delta t_i}{1 - \mu_i s_{Mi}} \tag{2.5}$$

From the Divisia definition of value-added growth Δv (equation (2.4)), equation (2.5) becomes:

$$\Delta v_i = \left[\frac{\mu_i(1 - s_{Mi})}{1 - \mu_i s_{Mi}}\right]\Delta x_i^V + \left[\frac{\mu_i s_{Mi}}{1 - \mu_i s_{Mi}} - \frac{s_{Mi}}{1 - s_{Mi}}\right](\Delta m_i - \Delta y_i) + \Delta t_i \frac{\Delta t_i}{1 - \mu_i s_{Mi}} \tag{2.6}$$

Equally, the expression for the primary input growth is as the weighted average of capital and labor, using shares in value added, hence yielding as:

$$\Delta x_i^V = \frac{s_{Ki}}{1 - s_{Mi}}\Delta k_i + \frac{s_{Li}}{1 - s_{Mi}}\Delta l_i \equiv s_{Ki}^V \Delta k_i + s_{Li}^V \Delta l_i \tag{2.7}$$

Given that, with imperfect competition, taking value-added as a function of primary inputs may indicate a mis-specification. In this model, I emulated BFK and model the growth rate of productive value added Δv^p as a revenue-weighted growth in primary inputs Δx^v, plus technology shocks and then normalise to one in the first period the elasticity of productive value added V^{vv} with respect to technology, hence I have:

$$\Delta v_i^p = \mu_i^V \Delta x_i^V + \Delta t_i \tag{2.8}$$

---

[33] See appendix A2.5

The implication is that, the value added mark-up μ_i^V is equal to the ratio of the price of productive value added and the marginal cost of producing it. Therefore, substituting into equation (2.4), the value added becomes:

$$\Delta v_i = \mu_i^V \Delta x_i^V + \left(\mu_i^V - 1\right)\left[\frac{s_{Mi}}{1 - s_{Mi}}\right]\left(\Delta m_i - \Delta y_i\right) + \Delta t_i \qquad (2.9)$$

Equation (2.9) implies that, the real value added growth would depend on the primary input growth, changes in materials-to-output ratio, and technology. The first term in the equation represents primary inputs multiply by the value added mark-up, while the second term indicates the extent to which the standard measure of value added would differ from the productive value added V^{Pi}. Since this does not adequately characterize measured productive contribution of intermediate inputs, its elimination using revenue shares is possible. If on the other hand, we assume the presence of imperfect competition, the productive contribution of these inputs would exceed the revenue share by the mark-up. The third term in equation (2.9) represents the value added augmenting technology shock. In which case, it is possible to define Δp_i as:

$$\Delta p_i = \left(\mu_i^V - 1\right)\Delta x_i^V + \left(\mu_i^V - 1\right)\left[\frac{s_{Mi}}{1 - s_{Mi}}\right]\left(\Delta m_i - \Delta y_i\right) + \Delta t_i \qquad (2.10)$$

The reasoning for this specification is that, firm-level productivity growth measured in terms of value added would depend in part on the markups. Therefore, taking into consideration imperfect competition, the productivity growth would also depend positively on changes in the relative intensity of intermediate input use. Having established the estimation process at firm level, we can therefore, discuss on the aggregation application in this model but first, look at the firm level aggregation and then aggregation for technology.

2.2 The Aggregation over Firms Specification

The model aggregate estimation specification followed exactly the same approach used by BF (2002) and BFK (2006) for the US. I therefore, apply similar methodology in estimating the model for the UK economy (1970 – 2000). The reason for the period covered is because the Bank of England Industry Dataset 2003 (BEID hereafter) used extended only to 2000. Equally, I also assume that technology shocks impacts on the measured aggregate productivity. Therefore, from the production side of the national accounts identity, we define aggregate output with reference to Divisia index of firm-level value added, in growth rates as:

$$\Delta v = \sum_{i=1}^{N} w_i \Delta v_i \tag{2.11}$$

The term w_i represents firm i share of nominal value added[34]. Therefore, from the definition of s_{Ki}^{V} and s_{Li}^{V}, including the differentiation of aggregate K and L, aggregate primary input becomes:

$$\Delta x^{v} = \sum_{i=1}^{N} w_i \Delta x_i^{V} - R_K - R_L \tag{2.12}[35]$$

Where $R_K = \sum_{i=1}^{N} w_i s_{Ki}^{V} \left[\dfrac{P_{Ki} - P_K}{P_{Ki}} \right] \Delta k_i$, $P_{Ki} = P_K / \sum_{i=1}^{N} x$ (i.e. the reallocation term for capital), and

$$R_L = \sum_{i=1}^{N} w_i s_{Li}^{V} \left[\dfrac{P_{Li} - P_L}{P_{Li}} \right] \Delta l_i, \quad P_{Li} = P_L / \sum_{i=1}^{N} x \quad \text{(Reallocation for labor)}$$

Note: x is the number of sectors in the economy under consideration.

Equation (2.12) shows the aggregate primary-input growth Δx^{V} in terms of the weighted average of firm-level input growth and reallocations of capital and labor. Therefore, by substituting equation (2.11) into (2.12),

---

[34] That is $w_i = \dfrac{P^v V_i}{P^v V}$ or, $\dfrac{P_k K}{P_V Y} + \dfrac{P_L L}{P_V Y}$

[35] Equation (2.9) is derived as follows: $\Delta x^v = \sum_{i=1}^{N} w_i s_{Ki}^{V} \dfrac{P_K}{P_{Ki}} \Delta k_i + \sum_{i=1}^{N} w_i s_{Li}^{V} \dfrac{P_L}{P_{Li}} \Delta l_i$

$= \sum_{i=1}^{N} w_i (s_{Ki}^{V} \Delta k_i + s_{Li}^{V} \Delta l_i) - \sum_{i=1}^{N} w_i s_{Ki}^{V} \left[\dfrac{P_{Ki} - P_K}{P_{Ki}} \right] \Delta k_i - \sum_{i=1}^{N} w_i s_{Li}^{V} \left[\dfrac{P_{Li} - P_L}{P_{Li}} \right] \Delta l_i$

and taking note of the definition of firm-level productivity as in equation (2.10) that is, $\Delta p_i = \Delta v_i - \Delta x_i^V$ we have aggregate productivity as:

$$\Delta p = \sum_{i=1}^{N} \Delta p_i + R_K + R_L \tag{2.13}$$

Before we used equation (2.13) in the estimation, I further disaggregate the value-added, the estimated Δp residual and then multiply both before aggregating. The levels of the series were normalised to 1.0 in 1970 and accumulate the estimated growth rates. In terms of the reallocation variable, it may represent mis-measurement of inputs due to unobserved heterogeneity (see the appendix on endogeneity). For example, workers may not have identical observable characteristics even if they are of the same sex, age and/or education. In which case it is appropriate to define aggregate productivity as the weighted average of firm-level productivity shocks, plus reallocation of capital and labor among uses with different shadow values. The other reasoning behind this is that, shifting resources to more highly valued users could lead to an increase in aggregate productivity even though firm-level productivity remained the same (see Stiglitz and Driffill 2000). Any deviation between aggregate productivity and aggregate technology may also be due to differences between firm-level productivity and firm-level technology.

Therefore, by substituting equation (2.12) for Δp_i the firm-level value added growth and rearranging, we have the expression for aggregate productivity in terms of aggregate inputs, reallocation of resources and aggregate technology, as follows:

$$\Delta p = \sum_{i=1}^{N} w_i(\mu_i^V - 1)\Delta x_i^V + \sum_{i=1}^{N} w_i\left(\mu_i^V - 1\right)\left[\frac{s_{Mi}}{1 - s_{Mi}}\right](\Delta m_i - \Delta y_i) + R_K + R_L$$

$$+ \sum_{i=1}^{N} w_i \Delta t_i \qquad\qquad\qquad (2.14)^{36}$$

The model specification uses markup term as a proxy for the control for imperfect competition. To see clearly how this works, we can examine some of the implications in the next section. Understanding their impacts will also help explain why this study is important.

2.3.1 The implications of the markup terms

The markup-reallocation has considerable implications on the productivity level estimations. The markups in the model played an essential role because; it acted as the control for imperfect competition. This is because the mark-up denoted as R_μ acted as a channel of access for shifting resources to users with higher social valuations. In which case, it is the wedge between social valuations of goods, that is, its price and the marginal cost. In table 2.1 below, I show the estimated sectoral markups used in the TFP. The level of markups varied across sectors, with the highest being 2.010 and the lowest 1.00. We can now examine the data used in the estimations in the next section.

2.3.2. The Welfare Implication

The view as expressed in BF (2002) is that a slightly modified Solow productivity residual measures changes in economic welfare. This is irrespective of whether productivity and technology are different, which is feasible as we will explore in greater details throughout this thesis.

---

[36] Aggregate productivity, can also be shown as technology, aggregate inputs and reallocations:

$$\Delta p = \left(\overline{\mu}^v - 1 \right) \Delta x^v + R_\mu + R_M + \overline{\mu}^v R_K + \overline{\mu}^v R_L + \Delta t$$

where, $\overline{\mu}^v = \sum_{i=1}^{N} w_i \mu_i^v$, $R_\mu = \sum_{i=1}^{N} w_i \left(\mu_i^v - \overline{\mu}^v \right) \Delta x_i^v$, and $R_M = \sum_{i=1}^{N} w_i \left(\mu_i^v - 1 \right) \left[\frac{s_{Mi}}{1 - s_{Mi}} \right] \Delta y_i$

$\Delta t = \sum_{i=1}^{N} w_i \Delta t_i$

This equation highlights the difference existing between aggregate productivity and aggregate technology.

The difference or gap between the two reflects imperfect competition. Furthermore, BF (2002) regarded the gaps as important and therefore estimated the average sectoral markups. Their findings suggests that the usual concentration on one sector dynamic general equilibrium models fails to consider an essential propagation mechanisms that are present only in multi-sector models.

The model implies that when productivity is computed from aggregate data, it has a natural welfare implication. Therefore, the modified Solow residual, which reduces to Solow's residual where there are no economic profits becomes a measure of welfare change for a representative consumer. Moreover, it shows that productivity instead of gross domestic product (GDP) is the appropriate measure of economic welfare. Productivity can shift in the short term for reasons unrelated to technology change. This can be illustrated by using identical households to solve the following intertemporal problem:

Maximize $U = \sum_{s=0}^{\infty} \beta^s u\left(C_{1,t+s}, C_{2,t+s}, C_{N-1,t+s}, \bar{L} - L_{t+s}\right)$ subject to

$$A_{t+1} = A_t + P_{Lt}L_t + P_{Kt}K_t - P_{t+1}^I K_t + \left(P_{t+1}^I - P_t^I\right)K_t + r_t B_t + \Pi_t - \sum P_{i,t}C_{i,t} \quad (2.15)$$

Where A is holds assets, taken to be the sum of private consumption bonds, B (with price normalized to 1) and capital K depreciating at rate δ. The term L denotes labour, $\bar{L}$ is each consumer's per period endowment of labour while P^I is the price of investment goods, P_{Kt} is the rental price of capital and P_{Lt} is the real wage. This assumes that all producers pay homogenous inputs the same factor price. That is, for any input J and firm i $P_{Jit} = P_{Jt}$. The rate of return of bonds is r and pure profits are rebated lump-sum to consumers. Therefore in equilibrium, $B_t = 0$ for all t and $\left(1 + r_t\right)P_{Kt} = \left(1 + r_t\right)P_t^I - \left(1 - \delta\right)P_{t+1}^I$. This assumes that capital is paid in the same period that it is rented, thus complies with empirical literature on cyclical productivity (BF, (2002), Hall, (1990)).

Assuming λ to be the shadow value of assets at time t, the consumer's first order conditions will be as follows:

$$u_{L_t} = \lambda_t w_t ,$$

$$u_{C_{i,t}} = \lambda_t P_{i,t} \qquad i = 1,...,N-1 \tag{2.16}$$

And together with the Euler equation as:

$$\lambda_t = \beta(1+r_t)\lambda_{t+1} \tag{2.17}$$

It follows that a temporary shock at time t can change output, consumption and labour supply. The shock will imply a change in technology, market structure (that is, markups of price over marginal cost) and government expenditure. Thus, to a first approximation, the perturbation changes lifetime utility by:

$$\Delta U = \sum_{i=1}^{N-1} u_{C_{i,t}} \Delta C_{i,t} - u_{L_t} \Delta L_t + \beta \lambda_{t+1} \Delta A_{t+1}$$

$$\lambda_t \left[\sum_{i=1}^{N-1} P_{i,t} \Delta C_{i,t} - P_{Lt} \Delta L_t \right] + \beta \lambda_{t+1} \Delta A_{t+1} . \tag{2.18}$$

Therefore, from the national income identity[37], the change in the value of consumption in terms of changes in aggregate output and investment can be expressed as:

$$\sum_{i=1}^{N-1} P_{i,t} \Delta C_{i,t} = P_t^C C_t \left[\sum_{i=1}^{N-1} \frac{P_{i,t} C_{i,t}}{P_t^C C_t} \frac{\Delta C_{i,t}}{C_{i,t}} \right]$$

$$= P_t^V V_t \frac{\Delta V_t}{V_t} - P_t^I \Delta I_t . \tag{2.19}$$

---

[37] The national income identity is: $\Delta v = \frac{P^C C}{P^V V} \left[\sum_{i=1}^{N-1} \frac{P_i C_i}{P^C C} \frac{\Delta C_i}{C_i} \right] + \frac{P^I I}{P^V V} \frac{\Delta I}{I}$, where $P^C C = \sum_{I=1}^{N-1} P_i C_i$ is nominal expenditure on consumption goods, $P^I I$ is nominal expenditure on the investment good and $P^V V = P^C C + P^I I$ is total nominal output.

The capital stock at time $t-1$ is predetermined when the shock occurs at time t, the change in investment at time t is also the change in the time t capital stock: $\Delta I_t = \Delta K_t$. Therefore, combining equations (2.17) and (2.19), while noting that capital is the only asset, equation (2.18) can be rewritten as:

$$\Delta U = \lambda \left[P_t^V V_t \frac{\Delta V_t}{V_t} - P_t^I \Delta K_t - P_{Lt} \Delta L_t \right] + \beta \lambda_{t+1} \Delta A_{t+1}$$

$$\lambda_t \left[P_t^V V_t \frac{\Delta V_t}{V_t} - P_t^I \Delta K_t - P_{Lt} \Delta L_t + \frac{(1-\delta) P_{t+1}^I}{1+r_t} \Delta K_t \right]. \tag{2.20}$$

Thus, simplifying by taking $P^V V$, outside the brackets and rearrange in logarithmic form yields:

$$\Delta U = \left(\lambda_t P_t^V V_t \right) \left[\Delta v_t - \frac{P_{Kt} K}{P_t^V V_t} \Delta k_t - \frac{P_{Lt} L_t}{P_t^V V_t} \Delta l_t \right]$$

$$= \left(\lambda_t P_t^V V_t \right) \Delta p_t. \tag{2.21}$$

The above equation (2.21) means that the change in utility is proportional to the change in the modified Solow residual Δp_t. In other word, the welfare change of any one period shock at time t is equivalent to having an exogenous increase in national income of Δp percent at time t, which is then added to the consumer's assets. The welfare gain is proportional to productivity growth and not to output growth because the consumer subtracts the welfare cost of supplying any extra capital and labour.

According to BF (2002), aggregate data yields a useful measure of welfare change because the welfare properties of the Solow residual follow from the equality of relative market prices to the consumer's marginal rates of substitution (MRS) between goods. In other words, it includes the equality of the real wage to the MRS between goods and leisure.

2.4   Data Analysis and methodology

In the model, the measure of aggregate technology change Δt used contrasted with aggregate productivity growth Δp. I initially estimated technology change at disaggregated level and then aggregate. This methodology also relates to Hall (1988) and Hindriks et al (2000).

I used the BEID (2003) dataset. The dataset comprises of annual data on 34 industries sector covering the whole economy from 1970 – 2000. The main variables are gross output, value added, capital, labour and intermediate input. The BEID capital input computation came from the services of seven assets, of which three are ICT (computers, Software and communications equipment). Each industry's intermediate input is an aggregate of purchases from all other industries and from imports. The labour input is measured by hours worked but with an adjustment for quality change derived from aggregate data. The dataset construction is consistent with the national accounts, both in nominal and real terms. It is also consistent with the 2002 Blue Book. An important principle behind the BEID dataset is that industry output are measured gross, so that proper account can be taken of the contribution of intermediate input.

The data for the instruments used are from SPIRI, Jenkins defence, OECD, and the Bank of England. The other instruments used are Oil from OPEC & WDS_IEA (crude oil spot prices) and Political based on the periods the Conservative Party or Labour Party is in power.

My aggregation covered the U.K economy of which full dataset was available. I decided only to study the U.K due to limited availability of data for other countries. I replicated the BF (2002) paper for the US economy but did not include it in this thesis. In that exercise, I used the dataset of BF (2002), provided to me by John Fernald. For this thesis, the capital share s_K was computed by the Bank of England for each industry by constructing a series for required payments to capital following Hall (1990), and BF (2002).

2.4.1   Data

2.4.1A.   Output: Nominal output

The accounting identity relating to gross output and value added in nominal terms is:

Gross output = Value added + Domestic intermediate input + Imported intermediate input. In addition, the definition for value added is as follows:

Value added = Gross operating surplus (profits) + Wage bill + Taxes on production[38].

Value added is at basic prices.

Real output

The BEID dataset define nominal gross output as the sum of nominal value added and nominal intermediate input, a Divisia index or real gross output in industry i is:

$$\hat{Y}_i = v_i \hat{V}_i + (1 - v_i)\hat{M}_i$$

Therefore;

---

[38] Nicholas Oulton and Sylaja Srinivasan, (2003); the Bank of England Industry Dataset

$$\hat{V}_i = [\hat{Y}_i - (1 - v_i)\hat{M}_i] / v_i \qquad (2.22)$$

Where Y_i is real gross output in industry, i, V_i is real double deflated, value added, M_i is real intermediate input, v_i is the share of nominal value added in nominal gross output, and a hat denotes a growth rate. Equation (2.22) defines the real value added that I used in the econometric modelling. See appendix A2.2 for full discussion on the Divisia Index.

Consistency of industry real output with official estimates of GDP growth

The BEID dataset considered the two ways to measure real GDP, from output or from expenditure. The output side uses a Divisia index of GDP growth:

$$\Delta GDP = \sum_{i=1}^{n} w_i \hat{V}_i \qquad i.....n \qquad (2.23)$$

Where w_i is the share of nominal value added in industry i in aggregate nominal value added (current price GDP), and there are n industries while Δ is the GDP growth. From the expenditure side:

$$\Delta gdp = \sum_{i=1}^{n} s_i \hat{E}_i \qquad (2.24)$$

Here E_i is final expenditure on the products of industry i and s_i is the share of final expenditure on i in current price GDP. Ignoring the difference between market prices at which, expenditure is usually measured and basic prices at which output is normally measured, the two measures of GDP growth are equal. This is in the absence of errors or omissions in the statistics. Equality exists only in principle if, value added is measured by double deflation as in equation (2.22)[39].

---

[39] For full detail see the BEID dataset (2003).

2.4.1B   Capital

The capital input in the BEID dataset is a measure of capital services from different types of assets. It also distinguishes between ICT and non-ICT capital. Oulton and Srinivasan (2003) provided full discussion of the methods and empirical considerations. They estimated for each of the 34 industries the capital services flowing from stocks of the following 4 non-ICT assets:

Buildings (excluding residential dwellings)

1. Equipment (excluding computers, part of software and communication equipment)
2. Vehicles
3. Intangibles (excluding rest of software)

And for the following 3 ICT assets:

1. Computers
2. Software
3. Communication Equipment

Furthermore, the view was that while the wealth measure of capital is more firmly established and the standard measure produced by the ONS, in the context of production theory the flow of capital services is the correct measure to use (see Oulton and Srinivasan (2003, section 1)).

The calculation for the ICT, non-ICT and total fixed capital were by weighting the growth of asset stocks in the respective categories by their rental prices. To obtain the rental prices, the BEID adopted the Hall-Jorgenson formula.

2.4.2   The Method

The equation for the estimated capital services were as follows:

$$B_{it} = I_{it} + (1 - \delta_i) \cdot B_{i,t-1}, \quad i = 1, \ldots, m \tag{2.25}$$

$$A_{it} = (1 - \delta_i / 2) \cdot B_{it} \tag{2.26}$$

Equations (2.25) and (2.26) provided the description of the measurement process for asset stocks. This is from the accumulation equation:

$$A_{it} = (1 - (\delta_i / 2)) \cdot I_{it} + (1 - (\delta_i / 2)) \cdot (1 - \delta_i) \cdot I_{i,t-1} + (1 - (\delta_i / 2)) \cdot (1 - \delta_i)^2 \cdot I_{i,t-2} + \ldots \tag{2.27}$$

Here, the factor $(1 - \delta_i / 2)$ came about because of the assumption investment is spread evenly throughout the unit period, thus on average it attracts depreciation at a rate equal to half the period rate. This assumption affects the level but not the growth rate of capital stock.

$$K_{it} = \overline{A}_{it} = [A_{i,t-1} \cdot A_{it}]^{1/2}, \tag{2.28}$$

Equation (2.28) implies that capital services during period t derived from assets in place in the middle of period t. The capital stock in the middle of period t is estimated as the geometric mean of the stocks at the beginning and end of the period, hence:

$$P_{it}^K = T_t [r_t \cdot p_{i,t-1}^A + \delta_t \cdot p_{it}^A - (p_{it}^A - p_{i,t-1}^A)] \tag{2.29}$$

Equation (2.29) defines the rental price of assets of type i.

$$\Pi_t = \sum_{i=1}^{m} P_{it}^K K_{it} = \sum T_{it} \cdot [r_t \cdot p_{i,t-1}^A + \delta_i \cdot p_{it}^A - (p_{it}^A - p_{i,t-1}^A)] \cdot K_{it} \tag{2.30}$$

Equation (2.30) indicates that capital share equals the sum over all assets of the rental price times the asset stock.

$$\ln[K_t / K_{t-1}] = \sum_{i=1}^{m} \overline{w}_{it} \ln[K_{it} / K_{i,t-1}]$$

$$\overline{w}_{it} = (w_{it} + w_{i,t-1}) / 2, w_{it} = \frac{P_{it}^K K_{it}}{\sum_{i=1}^{m} P_{it}^K K_{it}}, \quad i = 1, \dots, m \tag{2.31}$$

Finally, equation (2.31) defines the growth rate of capital services. The aggregation in this equation uses the Fisher index and not Törnqvist index. The variables definitions are as follows:

m = the number of assets

A_{it} = the real stock of the ith type of asset at the end of period t

$\overline{A}_{it}$ = the real stock of the ith type of asset in the middle of period t

B_{it} = the real stock of the ith type of asset at the end of period, t assuming investment is at the end of the period, instead of spread evenly through the period

K_{it} = real capital services from assets of type i during period t

I_{it} = the real gross investment in assets of type i during period t

δ_i = the geometric rate of depreciation on assets of type i

r_t = the nominal post-tax rate of return on capital during period t

T_{it} = the tax-adjustment factor in the Hall-Jorgenson cost of capital formula

P_{it}^K = the rental price of new assets of type i payable at the end of period t

P_{it}^A = the corresponding asset price at the end of period t

Π_t = capital share (= nominal aggregate capital services) in period t

K_t = real total capital services during period t

w_{it} = is the share of nominal value added in industry i in aggregate nominal value added (current GDP)

2.4.3 Labour

A possible accurate method to account for labour input is to measure it using hours worked, and make adjustment for labour quality. In other words, to break it into various types for example by age, sex and qualifications and measure aggregate labour as a weighted average of hours worked by each group. The weights are the shares of each type of labour in the aggregate wage bill. This assumes that a version of marginal productivity theory holds. That is, each type of labour payment is in proportion to its marginal product (Oulton and Srinivasan, (2003)). An ideal situation would be to construct a chain index of labour input for each industry, but this would require for each industry data on hours worked by age, sex and qualifications. According to BEID dataset, this is not possible for the U.K at the level of industry disaggregating.

The Bank relied on the employer-based surveys for head counts of number of people employed by industry. This meant, using the New Earnings Survey (NES) and the employer-based, for hours per worker, by industry. An alternative source for hours worked and for qualifications is the Labour Force Survey (LFS), which is a survey of households. The Bank made two aggregate level adjustments to the industry estimates; first, making the growth of aggregate hours consistent with the measure derived from the LFS (ONS code: YBUS). The second adjustment is to use an index of quality change constructed by the Bank staff (Burriel-Llombart and Jones (2003)), which is for the whole economy, and is a Törnqvist index encompassing the effects of changes in the composition of the labour force by age, sex and qualifications.

The labour input I used is the quality adjusted hours worked.

2.4.4 Intermediate input

Nominal input

The Bank used the purchases of the products of each of the original 49 industries from domestic sources and separately from imports. Hence, for each year there are 49 x 49 matrixes of domestic purchases and a 49 x 49 matrix of purchases from imports. The domestic / imports split used the input-output tables.

Real input

For each product, there is a domestic price index and an import price index. The deflation of purchases is through the price index. Then for each industry, the Bank constructed a Fisher index of aggregate domestic intermediate input and a Fisher index of aggregate imported intermediate input. The view was that given the problem of volatility in the index, the Bank adjusted it and then calculated a two-year, moving average of the growth rates that produces the 34-industry level as Fisher indices of the indices at the 49-industry level.

2.4.5. The Instrumental variables

In this sub section, I provide explanations as to the appropriateness of instruments used in the estimation. The required instruments needs to be uncorrelated with technology change (see also BF (1997). Therefore,

I used a version of the Hall-Ramsey instruments. That is, the growth rate of the price of oil deflated by the GDP deflator, the growth rate of real government defence expenditure, monetary policy and the political party of the government (or Prime Minister).

The null hypothesis of invariance is rejected by finding a positive correlation between the productivity residual and an exogenous instrument. This was done by calculating the regression coefficient of the productivity residual on the instrument and using the t-test for inference. The instrumental variables for the test should cause significant movements in employment and output but remain uncorrelated with the random fluctuations in productivity growth. The exogenous variables could occur through product demand or from factor supplies. Therefore, the absence of correlation with the random element of productivity growth means that, the instruments must not cause movements in productivity and also, must not respond to random variations in productivity growth.

Monetary Policy Shock

Following BFK (2004) and Burnside (1996), and CEV (1999) and included the estimated quarterly VAR monetary innovations as an instrument. The measured monetary policy innovations to the 3-month Treasury Bill Rate from a VAR with GDP, GDP Deflator, Consumer Price Index, £-Month Treasury Bill Rate and M0.

As stated by Hall, there are doubts on the exogeneity of all measures of monetary policy that are much correlated with output. In terms of the fiscal side, defence expenditure is arguably unresponsive to the current state of employment and output.

Defence Expenditure

Defence expenditure sometimes undergoes large fluctuations that do not appear to be driven by the business cycle or by variations in productivity. On the other hand, there is no reason to assume that increases in government purchases of certain products should shift the production function for the industries making those products. However, changes in military employment assists identify the equation through fluctuations transmitted via the labour market.

The World Oil Price

It can be assumed that the historical pattern of changes in the world price of oil has not been caused in any significant way by fluctuations in U.K. productivity growth. Equally, shifts in oil prices do not cause changes in productivity. This hypothesis is justifiable because changes in factor prices do not shift production functions in the short run. Therefore, under this hypothesis, the observed tendency for measured productivity to fall when oil prices rise is the result of the negative response of output to that rise.

The Political Party of the Prime Minister

The systematic differences in economic policies of the two main political parties have caused differences in rates of expansion of the industries both over time and across industries. Output of services, durables and regulated industries have risen noticeably faster under Labour than under the Conservatives. Under the reasonable hypothesis that neither party has adopted policies that affect productivity growth in the short run, this systematic difference can be used to test the joint hypothesis of competition and constant returns.

2.5 The Empirical Results

In this section, I provide the findings or results on the U.K 34 sectors that comprise the whole economy, including the manufacturing sectors. Table 2.2 is the list of sectors used in the research and their SIC92 numbers[40]. I estimated the non-technological terms from our accounting identity. As the emphasis is on aggregate productivity and technology, the use of industry data is appropriate. This complements firm-level studies of narrowly defined industries, see for example, Bertin et al (1995).

Figure 2.1 plots the measured productivity and technology growth rates during 1970 – 2000 for the UK economy. Although productivity and technology fluctuations are by no means identical, they have some similarities. The periods 1973-74, 1979-80 and 1982 – 83 are one of recessions. What followed next were periods of rapid recovery. The period 1987 – 89 was a boom, and subsequently a large crash in 1991 – 92. The next periods were another rapid recovery until 1995. Figure 2.1 also shows the aggregate fluctuations of productivity and technology from the estimated TFP for the UK economy. Prior to the estimations, the data were tested for stationarity. The purpose for checking the stationarity is to ensure its suitability before carrying out empirical estimations for TFP. This is to avoid the TFP estimation exploding.

---

[40] Tables A2.1 in the appendix section provides the list of industries in US (BF (2004)) and table A2.2 is the difference between BF U.S sectors and the BEID UK sectors.

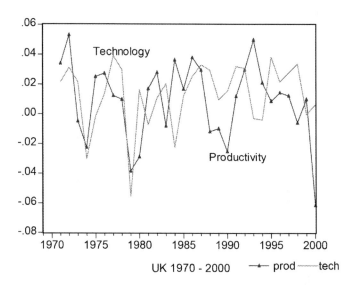

Figure 2.1: The Estimated UK Productivity and Technology Growth Rates

Intuitively, figure 2.1, shows that both productivity and technology co-moves; however, technology growth rate is slightly more fluctuating than productivity growth rate. The fluctuations on the technology growth rate exhibit shorter intervals than productivity growth rate. There is also a gap between the two growth rate series, which in this respect indicate an existence of a propagation mechanism. In addition, it is of similar behaviour in figure 2.2 below, which shows the levels of growth for the UK TFP.

In terms of the policy implications, this answers some of the research questions, especially, research question (1) and question (2). Fundamentally, since the level of productivity is sometimes above that of technology, it may well indicate that there are improvements or increased efficiency in the economy. More importantly, the gap between aggregate productivity and aggregate technology implies a strong presence of imperfect competition in the economy. Where there is a perfect competition, there will be no gap between them and the two will be the same. In the figures, aggregate productivity growth rates have been persistent over many period intervals since 1970. It shows the performance of the UK economy, for example, between the periods 1970 – 73, 1976 – 78, 1982 - 83, 1985 - 89, and 1992-95. Both productivity and technology seem to be on par from 1995 – 1997 before productivity growth level tends towards petering above technology again in 2000. One way to view the above results illustrated by our graphs is to understand that a temporarily adverse shock may make it advisable for firms to engage in some intertemporal labour substitution. Intertemporal substitution entails making trade-offs over time, postponing or bringing forward actions in the long-run plans of firms[41].

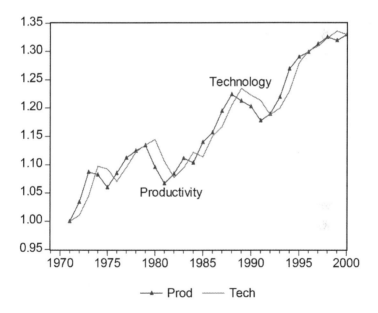

Figure 2.2: The Level of TFP in U.K: Aggregate Productivity and Aggregate Technology (normalised to one in 1970)

Figure 2.2 above shows the level of TFP for the whole U.K economy. The estimated TFP is equation (2.14), that is, aggregate productivity

---

[41] See for example Begg et al (2000), Economics, 6th edition, p531.

and aggregate technology. In figure (2.2), there appears to be a lag effect between aggregate productivity and aggregate technology. If there is a lag effect, then it would mean that aggregate technology is lagging aggregate productivity. This scenario implies that aggregate productivity is rising in response to increasing aggregate technology. Furthermore, this would comply with the discussion on RBC model in section (1.2.3) of chapter 1. It also shows that technology is the driving force propelling productivity increases. Another important aspect of the result is that, it shows imperfect competition among other factors has a dominant influence on aggregate productivity. This follows from our discussions in section 2.3 of this chapter. Given imperfect competition either in the product or factor markets, productivity and technology is likely to be different. This result goes to support Hall's (1988 and 1990) argument that with imperfect competition productivity rises when primary inputs of capital and labour increase. This of course would depend on the existence of a substantial gap between price and marginal cost at a representative firm. Imperfect competition affects productivity through the so called, Hall's "average" effect.

In addition, a factor's marginal product may differ across firms. In other words, firms may possess different degrees of market power in output markets, or pay different prices for the same inputs. For example, durable goods firms may have large mark-ups than non-durable goods firms. In addition, durable good industries are more cyclical, and as such tend to employ a larger share of the marginal inputs during boom periods than non-durable good industries. This marginal reallocation makes productivity cyclical even if technology does not change and even if the average sector has only a small markup.

The other effect is that, with imperfect competition, intermediate input use in general affects aggregate value added. Value added takes gross output and subtract intermediate inputs valued at their purchase price and not at their marginal product. The gross value added for a particular industry represents its contribution to national GDP. The assumption is that imperfect competition drives the wedge between prices and the marginal product of these intermediates. The wedge in this circumstance represents real goods and services. The average and the marginal product argument depend on the allocation of resources across uses and contribute to aggregate productivity. How effective this is would depend if the level of productivity at some interval exceeds the level of technology. Furthermore, sectoral shifts demand shocks may also cause differences in the marginal product of immobile factors across firms (Phelan and Trejos (2000)). Equally, within narrowly defined industries, productivity change often reflects reallocation of resources among firms with different levels of productivity – see Baily et al (1992).

Table 2.1: Sectoral Estimated Markups (1970 – 2000) – U.K

No.	SECTORS	SIC'92	μ^1	S.E	μ^2	S.E
1.	Agriculture	01,02,05	1.158	0.584	1.121	0.566
2.	Oil and gas	11,12	2.010	0.130	2.005	0.130
3.	Coal & mining	10,13,14	1.134	0.214	1.108	0.208
4.	Manufacture fuel	23	1.164	0.199	1.159	0.198
5.	Chemical & pharmaceuticals	24	1.553	0.482	1.558	0.486
6.	Non-metallic mineral products	26	1.149	0.531	1.116	0.501
7.	Basic metals & metal goods	27,28	1.307	0.332	1.295	0.331
8.	Mechanical engineering	29	1.000	0.442	1.000	0.450
9.	Electrical engineering & electronics	30,31,32,33	1.000	0.351	1.000	0.359
10.	Vehicles	34,35	1.217	0.250	1.243	0.257
11.	Food, drink & tobacco	15,16	1.000	0.633	1.000	0.592
12.	Textiles, clothing & leather	17,18,19	1.000	0.421	1.000	0.436
13.	Paper, printing and publishing	21,22	1.325	0.460	1.319	0.462
14.	Other manufacturing	20,25,36,37	1.431	0.592	1.391	0.557
15.	Electricity supply	40.1	1.405	0.310	1.396	0.306
16.	Gas supply	40.2,40.3	1.013	0.193	1.018	0.193
17.	Water supply	41	1.000	0.391	1.000	0.388
18.	Construction	45	1.217	0.472	1.234	0.475
19.	Wholesale, vehicle sales & repairs	50,51	1.459	0.445	1.469	0.453
20.	Retailing	52	1.695	0.821	1.836	0.870
21.	Hotels & catering	55	1.152	0.330	1.077	0.307
22.	Rail transport	60.1	1.042	0.248	1.045	0.247
23.	Road transport	60.2,60.3	1.000	0.375	1.000	0.362
24.	Water transport	61	1.000	0.248	1.000	0.246
25.	Air transport	62	1.194	0.213	1.196	0.213
26.	Other transport	63	1.000	0.314	1.000	0.327
27.	Communications	64	1.219	0.338	1.274	0.360
28.	Finance	65,66	1.523	0.825	1.436	0.775
29.	Business services	67,70,71,72,73,74	1.279	0.506	1.173	0.467
30.	Public administration and defence	75	1.000	0.428	1.000	0.401
31.	Education	80	1.000	0.708	1.000	0.162
32.	Health and social work	85	1.000	0.295	1.000	0.310
33.	Waste treatment	90	1.000	0.468	1.000	0.467
34.	Miscellaneous	91-99	1.000	0.140	1.000	0.138

Note: The term μ is the estimated markup. For μ^1, the labour input used is quality adjusted, while for μ^2 the labour input used is not quality adjusted. Both sets of data are from the BEID.

In the estimated markups used reported in table 2.1 above, all the estimated markups below 1 were replaced by 1 in the aggregation procedure. The estimated markup approach in this research assisted in providing a focus on technology against productivity.

2.6 Conclusions

In conclusion to this chapter, we can postulate that aggregate productivity and aggregate technology differs as demonstrated by the graphs above (figures 2.1 and 2.2). They are both different because of improvements in technology or increased efficiency. For policy implication purposes, the conclusion thereof is useful for distinguishing the impulses behind real business cycle.

By applying the approach in this chapter in the next chapter, it will enable this study to determine if the impulse responses are in conformity with the real business cycle (RBC) predictions. In RBC models, Solow's productivity residual (TFP) were used. However, in its interpretation, the assumption is that technology shocks are the dominant impulse during the cycle – see for example Cooley and Prescott (1995).

In addition, with reference to Barro and King (1984), the positive co-movement of output and labour input. The dynamic general equilibrium models without technology shocks can also match this stylised fact with counter-cyclical mark-ups of prices over marginal costs, which arises from sticky prices as in Kimball (1995) or from game theoretic firm interactions as in Rotemberg and Woodford (1992).

Furthermore, in models with increasing returns that is, increasing marginal product of labour can produce a positive co-movement between output and labour input. For example, see Farmer and Guo (1994). The other aspect is that if firms are not all perfectly competitive, using Solow residual as a measure of technology shocks mixes the impulse responses and propagation mechanisms. In this model, the assumption is that technology change is a dominant impulse; in other words technology has a permanent effect. For example, according to Burnside and Eichenbaum (1996), the postulation was that variable capital utilization rates are quantitatively important source of propagation to business cycle shocks.

In addition, the perception is that markups can either increase or reduce productivity, but the changes are likely to be relatively small. This can help explain why our graphs (figures 2.1 and 2.2), shows productivity and technology overlapping each other at intervals. It also shows that there is a higher level of output distribution and consumption, which does not alter the changes in technology.

No.	Sectors	SIC92
	Table 2.2: List of industries and their definitions – U.K	
1.	Agriculture	01,02,05
2.	Oil and gas	11,12
3.	Coal & mining	10,13,14
4.	Manufacture fuel	23
5.	Chemical & pharmaceuticals	24
6.	Non-metallic mineral products	26
7.	Basic metals & metal goods	27,28
8.	Mechanical engineering	29
9.	Electrical engineering & electronics	30,31,32,33
10.	Vehicles	34,35
11.	Food, drink & tobacco	15,16
12.	Textiles, clothing & leather	17,18,19
13.	Paper, printing and publishing	21,22
14.	Other manufacturing	20,25,36,37
15.	Electricity supply	40.1
16.	Gas supply	40.2,40.3
17.	Water supply	41
18.	Construction	45
19.	Wholesale, vehicle sales & repairs	50,51
20.	Retailing	52
21.	Hotels & catering	55
22.	Rail transport	60.1
23.	Road transport	60.2,60.3
24.	Water transport	61
25.	Air transport	62
26.	Other transport	63
27.	Communications	64
28.	Finance	65,66
29.	Business services	67,70,71,72,73,74
30.	Public administration and defence	75
31.	Education	80
32.	Health and social work	85
33.	Waste treatment	90
34.	Miscellaneous services	91-99

Source: Bank of England Industry Dataset

Note: SIC92 is the 1992 version of the U.K Standard Industrial Classification. The classification is identical to the European NACE system. Details on the SIC92 industry codes is available on http://www.statistics.gov.uk/methods_quality/sic/contents.asp

Appendix to chapter 2

Appendix A2.1

A2.1: Note: $F_T^i T_i / F^i = 1 - \mu_i s_{mi}$ that is, one less the mark-up times the intermediate input share. The term Δt_i is obtained from dividing Δy by $F_T^i T_i / F^i$.

A2.2: To show that the growth rate of value added Δv is in terms of primary inputs and intensity of intermediate-input use to equation (2.3) as in BF (1997), the derivation is as follows:

$$\Delta y_i = \mu_i (1 - s_{Mi}) \left[\frac{s_{Li}}{(1 - s_{Mi})} \Delta l_i + \frac{s_{Ki}}{(1 - s_{Mi})} \Delta k_i \right] + \mu_i s_{Mi} \Delta m_i + \frac{F_T^i T_i}{F^i} \Delta t_i$$

$$\mu_i (1 - s_{Mi}) \left[s_{Li}^V \Delta l_i + s_{Ki}^V \Delta k_i \right] + \mu_i s_{Mi} \Delta m_i + \frac{F_T^i T_i}{F^i} \Delta t_i$$

$$\mu_i (1 - s_{Mi}) \Delta x_i^V + \mu_i s_{Mi} \Delta m_i + \frac{F_T^i T_i}{F^i} \Delta t_i$$

A 2.3: By subtracting $\mu_i s_{Mi} \Delta y_i$ from the two sides, and dividing through by $(1 - \mu_i s_{MI})$, give the output growth as:

$$\Delta y_i = \left[\frac{\mu_i (1 - s_{Mi})}{1 - \mu_i s_{Mi}} \right] dx_i^V + \left[\frac{\mu_i s_{Mi}}{1 - \mu_i s_{Mi}} \right] (\Delta m_i - \Delta y_i) + \frac{F_T^i T_i}{F^i} \frac{\Delta t_i}{1 - \mu_i s_{Mi}}.$$

A 2.4: The primary input growth in this case is a weighted average of capital and labour, using shares in value added.

$$\Delta x_i^V = \frac{s_{Ki}}{1 - s_{Mi}} \Delta k_i + \frac{s_{Li}}{1 - s_{Mi}} \Delta l_i \equiv s_{Ki}^V \Delta k_i + s_{Li}^V \Delta l_i$$ A2.5: The value added in expanded form will be as follow:

$$\Delta v_i = \left[\frac{\mu_i (1 - s_{Mi})}{1 - \mu_i s_{Mi}} \right] \Delta x_i^V + \left[\frac{\mu_i s_{Mi}}{1 - \mu_i s_{Mi}} - \frac{s_{Mi}}{1 - s_{Mi}} \right] (\Delta m_i - \Delta y_i) + \frac{F_T^i T_i}{F^i} \frac{\Delta t_i}{1 - \mu_i s_{Mi}}$$

A2.6: $\sum_{i=1}^{N} w_i (\mu_i^V - 1) \Delta x_i^V = (\bar{\mu}^V - 1) \sum_{i=1}^{N} w_i \Delta x_i^V + \sum_{i=1}^{N} w_i (\mu_i^V - \bar{\mu}^V) \Delta x_i^V$

$$=\left(\bar{\mu}^V-1\right)\Delta x^V+\sum_{i=1}^{N} w_i\left(\mu_i^V-\bar{\mu}^V\right)\Delta x_i^V+\left(\bar{\mu}^V-1\right)\left(R_K+R_L\right)$$

Appendix A2.2: The Divisia Index

In our econometric model of TFP, aggregate productivity and aggregate technology equation is a derivation from the standard Divisia definition of firm level value added (Δv_i). I have therefore used here Hulten (1973) and Diewert (1988) studies to examine the rationale behind the adoption of Divisia index. Further more, Hulten (1973) related the Divisia index to economic price and quantity index under the assumptions of optimizing behaviour and a linearly homogenous aggregator function. Diewert (1988) on the other hand, postulates that the "derivation of the Divisia indexes are very mechanical and are unrelated to economics that is choice under constraint".

The Divisia Index (D.I) provided a method for indexing technical change (Solow 1957, Hulten 1973) hence, the widely utilization of it in studies involving measurement of productivity change. Examples of such studies can be found in, Denison (1962), Kendrick (1961), Jorgenson and Griliches (1967), and Christensen and Jorgenson (1970). The limiting factor to (D.I) is the multiplicity of index values because of the possibility of linkable with any given point in the set of variables during indexation. In addition, the DI is a line integral and as such can cycle over a given path. The solution to the cyclicality is to link with the economic theory of aggregation, thereby giving a condition where the DI is path independent (non-cyclical). Under this condition, the DI conserves all the information in the problem up to an arbitrary normalization. The effectiveness of the DI is that it is both paths independent and invariant. Thus, the **definition of Divisia index as the weighted sum of growth rates, where the weights are the components shares in total value.** For example, let us assume that $X_1^t\ldots\ldots X_n^t$ is the set of observations for indexation (that is the quantity q) and P_1^t.............P_n^t is the associated price vector, while α^t denote the path of the Xs over the time interval (O, T). Therefore, the DI in its continuous gives the form:

$$D(\Gamma) = \exp\{\int (\sum_{i=1}^{n} \frac{P_i^t X_i^t}{\sum_j P_j^t X_j^t} \frac{\dot{X}_i^t}{X_i^t})\}$$ (A2.2.1)

$$= \exp \{\int_{\Gamma} \phi.\partial\alpha^t\}$$

The dot over a variable denotes derivatives with respect to time, ϕ is the vector of prices normalized by the value shares, that is; $\phi = (\frac{P_1^t}{\sum P_j^t X_j^t}\cdots,\frac{P_n^t}{\sum P_j^t X_j^t})$ and Γ is the curve described by $\alpha^t, 0 \leq t \leq T$. The Divisia index in this case is the mapping of paths α^t into the real time. Note $\dot{X}_i^t / X_i^t$ can be replaced by $\dot{P}_i^t / P_i^t$ because the Divisia price index is dual to the quantity index. Equally, as the index is a line integral, it depends also on the path over which the integration is taking. In which case, if for ϕ continuous on S and x and y are two points on S, then we have:

$$\int_{\Gamma(x,y)} \phi.\partial\alpha = \int_{\Gamma_1(x,y)} \phi.\partial\beta$$ (A2.2.2)

In equation (A2.2.2) above, the paths are denoted by α, β describes the curves Γ and Γ_1, so that $\Gamma \subset S, \Gamma_1 \subset S$, and $\alpha \in \Gamma, \beta \in \Gamma_1$. Where equation (A2.2.2) is not satisfied, the line integral is part dependent. Equally, cycling does not exist if and only if the Divisia integral is independent of the path in $S \subset R^n$ (see Hoy et al 2001). This happens if there is an economic aggregate associated with each point { X_1^t.............$X_n^t\} \in S$. this implies that, to have a Divisia index of capital stock with non-cycling, the capital aggregate must exist. Although this is not a necessary or sufficient condition, further assumptions are therefore required to obtain a necessary and sufficient condition. The first assumption is that there is an existence of an aggregate as defined in S. The second assumption is the linear homogeneity of this aggregate, whilst the third is the existence of an (observable) price normal at each point in S, and unique up to a scalar multiplication. With these assumptions, the Divisia index (equation A2.2.1) is independent of the path of integration in S.

Two important facts emerge from this, which justifies both the assumption and our normalization of aggregate productivity and aggregate technology in the econometric modelling. First, if we assume that the variables in the index problem $\{X_1^t,.........X_n^t\}$, are subset of a larger number of variables $\{X_1^t,.........X_m^t\}.m \succ n$. Then the requirement, of an existence of aggregate, indicates that any function containing all m variables will be weakly separable into a function of the n variables in the index problem and a function of the other n – m variables. In terms of technology using capital and labour inputs, a Divisia index of capital, which is path independent, requires the assumption of weak separable on the production function (condition assumption 1). The second fact relates to the values taken by the index. Under condition assumption 3, the Divisia index retrieves the actual values of the aggregating function, subject to an arbitrary normalization in some base period. Hence, the Divisia index preserves up to the normalization, all the information in the problem.

The significance of this result relates to the discrete counterpart of condition assumption 1. The economic data used in this study take the form of observations at discrete points in time. The derivation of the relevant form of the index is therefore from

$$\log(D_t) - \log(D_{t-1}) = \sum_{i=1}^{n} \frac{1}{2}[V_{i,t} + V_{i,t-1}][\log(X_{i,t}) - \log(X_{i,t-1})], \text{ (A2.2.3)}$$

Where $V_{i,t} = \dfrac{p_{i,t}X_{i,t}}{\sum_{j}^{n} p_{j,t}X_{j,t}}$ (i = 1,....., n)

This is the rate of change of the discrete Divisia index, which is a computation from the observations on prices and quantities. It also approaches the continuous form (equation A2.2.1) as Δt goes to zero.

Therefore, under condition assumption 3, we can use the discrete Divisia index to approximate the true values of the underlying relationship on S. To simplify this, let us consider the Diewert (1988) approach. Equally in this approach, the Divisia index permits for a continuous change in price and quantity, taking into account the relation between the definition of price and quantity indices and total expenditure. Here, the Divisia generates the price and quantity indices by assuming that total expenditure function (v (t)) is continuous and differentiable. Therefore, the growth rate of aggregate price and quantity are as follows:

Assuming prices $p_i(t)$ and the quantities $q_i(t), i = 1, \ldots \ldots N,$ are functions of a continuous time t and expenditure at time t is the value $v(t) = \sum_{i=1}^{N} p_i(t) q_i(t)$, whilst differentiability, the rate of change of value at time t is:

$$\frac{\Delta v(t)}{\Delta t} = \sum_{i=1}^{N} p_i \left(\frac{\Delta q_i}{\Delta t} \right) + \sum_{i=1}^{N} q_i \left(\frac{\Delta p_i}{\Delta t} \right) \qquad \text{(A2.2.4)}$$

Dividing both sides of equation (A2.2.4) by $p(t) \bullet q(t) = \sum_{i=1}^{N} p_i(t) q_i(t)$ and setting the RHS of the resulting equation to $\frac{Q'(t)}{Q(t)} + \frac{P'(t)}{P(t)}$ where Q (t) and P (t) are aggregate quantity and price levels pertaining to period t, $Q'(t)$ and $P'(t)$ represents their time derivatives respectively. The expression $p(t) \bullet q(t)$ denotes an inner product that is, $x \cdot y = \sum_i x_i y_i$. The expression $\frac{Q'(t)}{Q(t)} + \frac{P'(t)}{P(t)}$ denotes growth rate of aggregate quantity and price levels respectively. Hence, we have:

$$\sum_{i=1}^{N} \frac{p_i q_i'(t)}{v(t)} + \sum_{i=1}^{N} \frac{q_i p_i'(t)}{v(t)} = \frac{Q'(t)}{Q(t)} + \frac{p'(t)}{p(t)} \cdot \qquad \text{(A2.2.5)}$$

The Divisia then defines Q (t) and P (t) as solutions to the following differential equations:

$$\frac{Q'(t)}{Q(t)} = \sum_{i=1}^{N} \frac{p_i(t) q_i'(t)}{p(t) \cdot q(t)}; \frac{p'(t)}{p(t)} = \sum_{i=1}^{N} \frac{q_i(t) p_i'(t)}{p(t) \cdot q(t)} \cdot \qquad \text{(A2.2.6)}$$

The expression $\dfrac{p_i(t) \cdot q_i(t)}{p(t) \cdot q(t)}$ denotes the shares of expenditure function, v (t) then given s_i is the ith expenditure share, then $s_i = \left[\dfrac{p_i(t) \cdot q_i(t)}{p(t) \cdot q(t)}\right]$, while the share of the growth rate of quantity is:

$$\frac{q'(t)}{q(t)} = \sum_{i=1}^{N} s_i \left[\frac{q_i'(t)}{q_i(t)}\right]$$

(A2.2.7)

Equation (A2.2.7) shows that the growth rate of aggregate quantity is the function of the summation of the product of expenditure share of firm or good i^{th} and its quantity growth rate. If we assume a zero profit, the equation corresponds to the concept of the equality between output and factor incomes, where $p_i(t)$ is the factor's price and $q_i(t)$ is the amount of factor i. It is possible to estimate the parameter s_i in this continuous function through econometric method while alternative method is the index number concept. According to Diewert (1976), assuming second-order approximation of transcendental logarithmic production function and using the quadratic estimation lemma, the index estimation is feasible through Törnqvist index. The discrete-time form of equation (A2.2.7) is:

$$\ln\left[\frac{Q(T)}{Q(T-1)}\right] = \sum_{i=1}^{N} \overline{s} \cdot \ln\left[\frac{q_i(t)}{q_i(t-1)}\right]$$

(A2.2.8)

where $\overline{s_i} = \dfrac{s_{i,t} + s_{i,t-1}}{2}$, that is, $\overline{s_i}$ represents the average cost share of each firm or good. It implies that if the LHS of equation (A2.2.8) indicates change in aggregate output and on the RHS, q_i and s_i denotes change in input and their income share of the aggregate output respectively. The difference between the two sides of the equation represents the residual or TFP.

Notes & Discussions

Notes & Discussions

Chapter 3

The Aggregate Productivity, Technology and Contractionary Effects

3.0 Introduction

In this chapter, the focus is on the estimation of aggregate productivity and technology with hours worked as a proxy. In chapter 2, the investigation concentrated on aggregate productivity and technology without the inclusion of hours (using the labor force instead). The introduction of a modified Solow residual or purified technology marks another distinction of this chapter from the previous chapter. Recapping from the previous chapters, we discussed how under imperfect competition, productivity is assumed to rise when primary inputs of capital and labor increases. Equally, factors may have different market powers in output markets for firms or different prices for the same input. However, changes in intermediate input use can affect aggregate output growth. For example, value added subtracts intermediate inputs valued at their purchase price rather than their marginal product. With imperfect competition, the marginal product would exceed the purchase price, thereby creating a wedge between real goods and services. At disaggregated level, the natural measure of firm output is the gross output. The real value added is just an artificial construct. We will see the effects on inputs in this chapter, as well as on other variables.

The attention in this chapter is to carry out disaggregate version of the regressions conducted in chapter 2. Technology is according to RBC an important source of business cycles and consequently the perception of its effect on employment as expansionary. This chapter henceforth follows closely the established BFK (2004) model approach. In the BFK model when technology improves upon impact, input use decreases while output changes very marginally. Among other studies, with results showing a reduction in total hours worked in the short run include Kiley (1998), Gali (1999), Francis and Ramey (2002). In Chang and Hong (2006), the effect on hours varied across industries, with some showing a reduction and others indicating a rise in hours. Shea (1999) also found an increase in input use especially labour in the short run. The BFK result therefore contradicts the prediction of real business cycle models of technology improvements being expansionary, that is, both inputs and output increasing instantaneously. I therefore apply the approach on UK economy (1970 – 2000) (disaggregated level) to examine if there are any contractionary effects, and if not, what could be the underlying causes.

The adopted approach allows for a focus on the construction of aggregate technology measurement. The development of time series techniques together with some identifying assumptions used to estimate the dynamic response of key macroeconomic variables to technology shocks in aggregate fluctuations are instrumental in this. These contributed to beneficial tools for assessing the sources of business cycle fluctuations and for constructing dynamic general equilibrium models (DGEM). The main problem in the process is how to identify shocks to technology.

A fundamental question in this empirical study is what kind of models would be consistent with the above scenario? This is bearing in mind that a standard one-sector real business cycle (RBC) model would not fit into the model because of the view of expansionary effects due to technology improvements. In addition, there is the assumption that inputs and outputs tends to rise instantaneously. Francis and Ramey (2001), as well as Vigfusson (2002) regard this view as consistent with the RBC models. The only drawback is it will require some modifications for preferences and technology, for example, habit formation and investment adjustment costs. Under this scenario, it would imply that a sticky-price approach could fit to solve the problem as it predicts that 'when technology improves, input use and investment demand would decline in the short term, including output'. Further more, in accordance with the standard RBC models, employment of capital and labour do rise in the short run when technology improves, while other macroeconomic models behave to the contrary. Since the measure for correlations would need appropriate measure of aggregate technology, I would follow in this case, BFK (2004) and construct a series by controlling for non-technological effects in aggregate total factor productivity (TFP) or the aggregate modified Solow residual[42].

The structure of this chapter is as follows: section 3.1 is the implication for real business cycles (RBC), and section 3.2 is the model approach to measurements. Section 3.3, is the results and 3.4, the conclusions.

3.1 The Implications for Real Business Cycles (RBC)

The findings from the various literatures discussed above are inconsistent with standard parameterizations of frictionless RBC model[43]. For instance, the BFK results seems to be in line with the predictions of DGE models with sticky prices, illustrated using the quantity theory and demand for money, with a fixed supply of money and sticky prices. According to the postulation, relaxing the quantity theory assumption

---

[42] This consists of varying utilization of capital and labour, non-constant returns and imperfect competition, and aggregation effects.
[43] This also includes King and Rebelo (1999).

would allow for a more robust dynamics for output and its components while maintaining the underlying principles.

Under sticky-price model, technology improvements can be feasible if the monetary authorities do not offset their short run effects through expansionary monetary policy. This is because of the prediction of full employment output creating a short run deflation, thereby facilitating lower interest rates[44]. The theoretical analysis of the sticky-price constitutes the discussion in the appendix to chapter 4 as well as reference to it in chapter 5. The reference to the sticky-price is important because of the role it played for example, BFK cited Marchetti and Nucci (2004)[45] in concluding that sticky prices are indeed responsible for their findings. In the meantime, we can in this section, look at the discussion in two parts, while leaving the sticky-price model scenario as discussed so far. In the next section, I will consider the firm level measurement.

These afore-mentioned procedures will enable us to achieve the objective of estimating aggregate technology using (instrumented) industry Hall-type regression equations with a proxy for utilization as in BFK (2004). By doing so, it will also be feasible to define aggregate technology change as the weighted sum of the resulting residuals.

---

[44] BFK (2004, p5) acknowledge other possibilities including flexible price with autocorrelation technology shocks, low capital-labour substitutability or substantial real frictions such as habit persistence in consumption and investment adjustment costs, sectoral shifts etc.

[45] Marchetti and Nucci (2004) applied BFK identification method to Italian firm-level data and found that technology improvements reduce input use (only at firms that have sticky prices); and a negative correlation between technology and hours.

3.2. The Model Approach

The model analysis starts with the assumption of firms possessing a gross output production function such as:

$$Y_i = F^i \left(A_i K_i, E_i H_i N_i, M_i, T_i \right). \tag{3.1}$$

In equation (3.1), Y_i represents the gross output, K_i is the capital stock, N_i denotes employees, M_i is the intermediate inputs (that is, energy and materials), H_i represents hours worked per employees, E_i denotes the effort per worker and A_i capital utilization rate or the capital's workweek. The terms $E_i H_i N_i$ forms the total labor input L_i. The capital stock together with the number of employees are assumed quasi-fixed. However, it is possible for firms to alter the intensity of inputs use. The term F^i is the firm's production function, which is homogeneous of arbitrary degree γ_i in total inputs. Where γ_i is greater than one, it will mean that the firm has increasing returns to scale, thereby reflecting overhead costs, decreasing marginal cost or both. The term T_i represents technology.

In this model, I follow BFK (2004) and Hall (1990) and assume the cost minimization approach by relating output growth to the growth rate of inputs. Therefore, the first order conditions yields the essential output elasticities, that is, the weights on growth of each input. Furthermore, the resulting estimating equation controls for imperfect competition and increasing returns. Thus, we can let Δx_i to be the observed input growth and Δu_i as the unobserved growth in utilisation. To conform to our model in chapter 2, Δv_i denotes value added productivity. In addition, for any variable J, I defined Δj as its logarithmic growth rate $\ln \left(J_t / J_{t-1} \right)$. I therefore have the following equations:

$$\Delta v_i = \gamma_i \left(\Delta \chi_i + \Delta u_i \right) + \Delta t_i, \tag{3.2}$$

Where

$$\Delta \chi_i = s_{Ki} \Delta k_i + s_{Li} \left(\Delta n_i + \Delta h_i \right) + s_{Mi} \Delta m_i ,$$ (3.3)

$$\Delta u_i = s_{Ki} \Delta a_i + s_{Li} \Delta e_i$$

And sj_i is the ratio of payments to input J in total cost.

Using a modified Solow residual or purified technology change[46], the weighted sum of industry technology change will become:

$$\Delta t = \sum_i \left(\frac{w_i}{1 - s_{Mi}} \right) \Delta t_i$$ (3.4)[47]

Furthermore, to weight the technology shocks by the firm's share of aggregate value added as in BFK, it would also mean adopting the Domar (1961) weighting procedure[48]. Finally, the output changes in firm-level utilization are from changes in aggregate utilisation. This therefore, represents the weighted average of firm-level utilization changes as:

$$\Delta u = \sum_i \left(\frac{w_i}{1 - s_{mi}} \right) \gamma_i \Delta u_i$$ (3.5)

Thus, to apply the methodology, we therefore require disaggregated estimates of returns to scale. Since in chapter 2, we relied on the use of μ_i, the markups in place of RTS, we therefore abstract from the estimation. The model measures utilization growth Δu_i as a weighted average of growth in capital utilization, A_i, and labour effort E_i. By linking capital hours and labor compensation by the shift premium, the disaggregated estimating equation that controls for input use would be:

---

[46] See appendix A3
[47] In equation (3.3), $w_i = (P_i Y_i - P_{Mi} M_i) / \sum_i (P_i Y_i - P_{Mi} M_i) \equiv P_i^v V_i / P^V V$, that is, the firm's share of aggregate nominal value added and by dividing with $1 - s_M$ transforms it into value added.
[48] See appendix A3.1

$$\Delta v_i = \mu_i \Delta x_i + \beta \Delta h_i + \Delta t_i \qquad (3.6)$$

The residual Δt_i denotes the industry technology, while the term β recognizes all the composite parameters in the coefficient that multiplies the term Δh_i and in effect, controls for capital and labour use. In addition, I restricted the estimation to within three groups: durables manufacturing; non-durables manufacturing and non-manufacturing. Therefore, for the industries within each group, the estimated equation is

$$\Delta v_i = c_i + \mu_i \Delta x_i + \beta \Delta h_i + \Delta t_i . \qquad (3.7)$$

Equation (3.7) controls for both capital and labor use. Hours per employee, growth $\beta \Delta h_i$ entered twice in the equation. This is because it is also in the observed input growth Δx_i. In addition, the inclusion of hours in the estimated equation distinguishes it from equation (2.14) in chapter 2. The estimated sectoral markups are in table 3.1 below. There are two groups of the markups: the manufacturing sector and the UK private economy (that is, excluding agriculture, education, health and social work, and public administration and defence). From the above estimation, the purified technology change Δt_i is the weighted sum of the industry residuals plus constant terms.

Capacity Utilization

Capacity utilization should be accounted for in the estimation of purified technology because of its definition in aggregate utilization as the contribution to final output of changes in firm level utilization, hence the equation (3.5) above. Furthermore, utilization growth Δu_i is a weighted average of growth in capital utilization, A_i and labour effort E_i. Given that cost-minimising firms operate on all margins simultaneously, changes in observed inputs can proxy for unobserved utilization changes with the relationship derived from the firm's first order conditions. Thus, changes in hours per worker are proportional to unobserved changes in both labor effort and capital utilization. The assumption is that firms minimise cost and are price takers in factor markets. Assumption about the firm's pricing and output behavior is not necessary.

In the next section are our results and our preliminary conclusions drawn from this chapter.

3.3   Results

The empirical results show the aggregate effects of technology shocks, estimated as an appropriately weighted average of industry regression residuals. I can now use the following graphs to explain the results.

Figure 3.1: Aggregate productivity and Technology

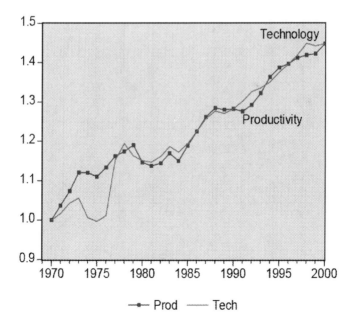

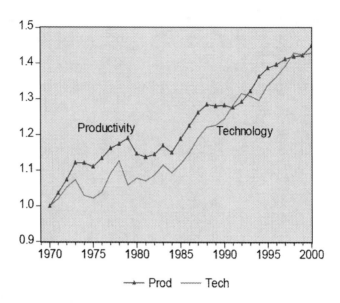

A: UK private business economy with hours

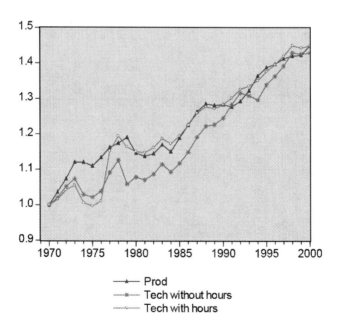

B: Private business economy without hours

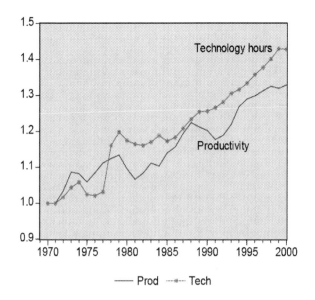

C: Prod, Tech and Tech hours (Private Economy)

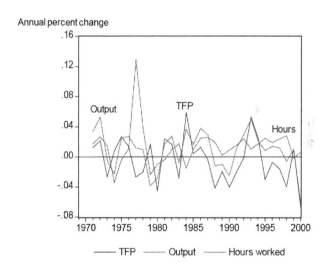

D: TFP whole Economy with Tech hours

Annual percentage change

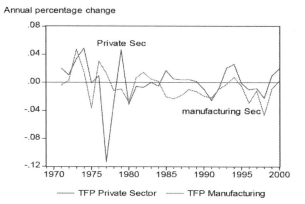

E: Percent changes in TFP,   F: Changes between private
Output & Hours   & manufacturing

Notes: The U.K sample period is 1969 – 2000. The series consists of the non-farm, non-mining private business economy. All the above graphs of figure 3.1 (A – F) are in growth rates.

In figure 3.1 (A), I show the aggregate productivity and aggregate technology level for the UK private business economy with hours, while 3.1 (B) is for the private business economy without hours. In figure 3.1 (C), I highlight the combinations for the level of productivity, technology and technology without hours. I used 3SLS method in the estimations for the level series in all of them. In figure 3.1 (A), there is a control for utilization, hence, both productivity and technology comoves much closer. In terms of utilization, this implies that firms are utilizing factors fully. In other words, if firms can costless change the rate of investment or hiring, they will always keep utilization at its long run cost-minimising level and vary inputs by hiring or dismissing workers and capital. Therefore, only if it is costly to adjust capital and labor is it necessary to pay the cost of varying utilization (BFK, (2004)). As can be seen from the figure, aggregate productivity and technology also overlap each other on intervals. One can refer to earlier discussion of this impact above.

In reference to the UK private business economy without hours in figure 3.1 (B), the gap between aggregate productivity and technology is much wider. In addition, aggregate productivity is consistently above aggregate technology. This explains our earlier assumptions about the driving force behind the propagation mechanism in TFP. In other words, one can refer to figure (2.1) in chapter 2, as to the lagging effects induced by technology, that is, technology being the driving force behind productivity rises. Equally, looking at figure 3.1 (C), the gap between the levels of the two forms of technology shocks is considerably wide. Technology hours is consistently well above technology without hours utilization control. It also positively comoves closer with productivity, especially from 1978 onwards.

Figure 3.1 (D) shows the level of aggregate productivity and technology for the whole UK economy with technology hours. It also shows technology hours consistently above productivity. As for figure 3.1 (E), it indicates the annual percentage changes in output, TFP and hours. The level of percentage changes in hours is consistently above that of output and TFP. The most significant change in hours is between 1976 and 1978. Priory to these periods, hours change lagged behind TFP and output, probably implying over capacity and inefficiency in the whole sectors of the UK economy. The changes between 1979 and 1981 saw a reversal of these inefficiencies syndrome within the whole economy. A possible explanation could be due to policy changes introduced by the authorities, especially on government industrial policy, industrial relations, labor laws and trade unions.

In figure 3.1 (E), the growth in aggregate output is measured as real value added while the growth in inputs is measured as the share-weighted average of growth in primary inputs of capital and labor. For TFP, the measure is output growth minus inputs growth. In all the series, technology refers to the utilization corrected aggregate residual. I have given the descriptions for the series in earlier discussions.

Furthermore, figure 3.1 (F) is the percentage changes in the private economy and the manufacturing sectors. The changes in the two sectors comove until 1976 when the private economy sectors suffered a huge negative change. However, since 1981, the percentage changes between them have been alternating with the private sector doing better than the manufacturing sector.

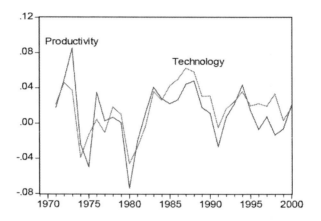

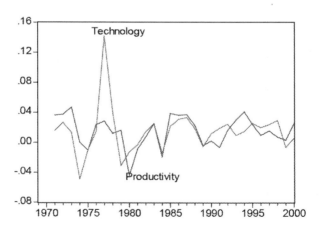

Figure 3.2: Aggregate Productivity and Technology percentage change in UK manufacturing sector (A) and B, the private economy.

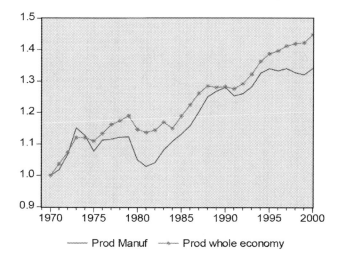

— Prod Manuf —*— Prod whole economy

Figure 3.2 (c): Aggregate Productivity Manufacturing and the whole economy

In Figure 3.2 (A), the graph displays the percentage change in aggregate production and technology for the manufacturing sector while in figure 3.2 (B), the graph shows that of the private sector. The aggregate fluctuations in (A) are on both series more prolonged and at a wider band change for manufacturing industries sector than in the private business economy sector (B). Furthermore, given that technology is the utilization corrected aggregate residual, it therefore shows what the true level of technology change should be if there is control for imperfect competition across the industry sectors. The measure of TFP depends on technology plus the change in utilization. The improvements in technology increases TFP, while a reduction is more likely to lead to its fall. In other words, on impact TFP increase less than the full increment in technology. In addition, figure 3.2c the aggregate productivity for the manufacturing sector and the level for the whole economy. The disaggregating in 3.2c is to show the level of productivity contribution of the manufacturing sector.

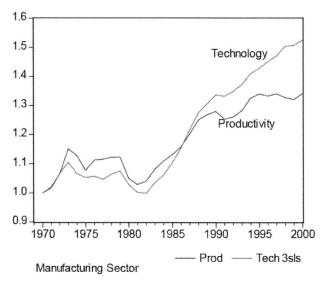

Figure 3.3: Aggregate Productivity and Technology in
manufacturing sector

Finally, figure 3.3 illustrates the results for aggregate productivity
and technology for the manufacturing sector. This shows technology
from the mid 1980s to be consistently above productivity signifying
a permanent effect increase within the economy. In table 3.1 below, I
provide a summary of the means and standard deviation of TFP from
OLS equation regression estimation.

Table 3.1: Summary of the Mean and Standard Deviation of TFP

		Private Economy	Manufacturing Economy
Solow Residual	Mean	0.014	0.011
	Std. Deviation	0.020	0.031
Purified Residual	Mean	0.014	0.017
	Std. Deviation	0.031	0.026
Hours	Mean	0.014	1.183
	Std. Deviation	0.027	0.139

Notes: U.K Sample period is 1969 – 2000. The purified technology is from aggregating residuals for the industries. Also included is the growth in hours per worker to control for unobserved utilization. The industry Domar weights are $w_i / (1 - s_{mi})$, where w_i, is the value added weight and s_{mi} is the share of intermediate inputs in output.

For the private economy, the standard deviation of technology 0.03 percent per year compares with the 0.02 percent standard deviation of TFP, a variance of 0.01 percent as low. It is also slightly similar result for hours. As for manufacturing, the standard deviation of technology is 0.026 percent per year compare with 0.031 percent of TFP, a variance of 0.01 percent per year as high. The reduction in variance is because of the decrease in positive covariance across industries, consistent with business cycle factors, common demand shocks that induce positive correlation changes in utilization and TFP across industries.

In table 3.2, I show the results of the estimated regression to a technology shocks Δt. The first row highlights the response with output growth changes, which is small on impact and negative after one-year lag. The second row is hours / utilization. The third row is the total observed inputs (cost-share weighted growth in capital and labor). On current technology, the effect is more on the manufacturing economy than it is on the private business economy. Furthermore, the recovery or the cyclical fluctuation is swifter in the manufacturing sector than it is in the private business sector. It is similar result on TFP especially on the manufacturing.

In terms of the impact-effect on hours or utilization when technology improves, it is insignificant. The impact on hours is a small decline after one year for the private economy but it recovers a little and positive in the second year, though not significant. However, sustaining the recovery is not possible as it went into contraction in the fourth year.

In terms of the economic implications, the observed response makes sense. It implies that, the initial response of labour input during a recovery reflects increased intensity. In other words, existing employees work longer and harder. As the recovery progresses, rising labour input hours in this case reflects primarily new employment rather than increased intensity.

Table 3.2: Regressions on Current and Lagged Technology

Dependent Variable (growth rate)	Δt	$\Delta t(-1)$	$\Delta t(-2)$	$\Delta t(-3)$	Δt (-4)	Cum Effects	R^2	S.E	D-W
Private									
Output	0.252	0.011	0.039	-0.199	-0.139	- 0.036	0.27	0.020	1.72
	(0.167)	(0.164)	(0.156)	(0.329)	(0.178)				
Input	0.546	0.466	0.295	0.322	0.407	2.036	0.311	0.027	1.52
	(0.260)	(0.245)	(0.231)	(0.224)	(0.225)				
Hours/utilisation	-0.037	-0.011	0.011	-0.029	-0.064	-0.13	•	0.005	2.06
	(0.047)	(0.041)	(0.040)	(0.042)	(0.043)				
Employment	-0.051	-0.021	0.132	-0.172	-0.192	-0.304	•	0.013	1.97
	(0.116)	(0.101)	(0.105)	(0.119)	(0.103)				
TFP	-0.878	0.081	0.054	-0.309	-0.038	-1.09	0.69	0.018	1.99
	(0.158)	(0.242)	(0.136)	(0.143)	(0.149)				
Manufacturing									
Output	1.061	0.015	-0.437	-0.024	0.098	0.713	0.81	0.014	1.93
	(0.146)	(0.149)	(0.142)	(0.142)	(0.121)				
Employment	0.164	0.277	0.055	-0.133	-0.104	0.259	0.61	0.013	1.81
	(0.154)	(0.151)	(0.159)	(0.160)	(0.122)				
TFP	0.153	-0.161	-0.291	0.071	0.003	-0.225	0.32	0.013	1.88
	(0.184)	(0.178)	(0.191)	(0.209)	(0.137)				
Input	-0.035	-0.027	0.012	0.031	0.013	-0.006	0.99	0.001	1.61
	(0.017)	(0.015)	(0.016)	(0.013)	(0.012)				
Hours/utilisation	0.027	0.035	0.029	-0.046	-0.060	-0.015	0.50	0.005	1.54
	(0.054)	(0.057)	(0.053)	(0.052)	(0.048)				

Notes: Each of the rows in table 3.3 represents a separate OLS regression of the variable shown in growth rates on the current value plus four lags of estimated technology growth, plus a constant term. The constant terms are not included in the table. The standard error is the parentheses in brackets. Sample adjustment: 1974 – 2000. I made some corrections for serial correlations in the estimations. The values of the DW-statistic showed evidence of serial correlations, hence the need for correction, by using lags of the dependent variables. The corrections however lowered the powers of the regressions coefficients.

The column with "cum effect" in table 3.2 is an aggregation of the shocks for that particular variable. For the private economy, both input and output showed a rise on impact following positive technology shocks, while hours, employment and TFP showed a decline or negative sign. For the manufacturing sectors, from the results in tables 3.2, only inputs have a negative sign on impact following a positive technology change, even though the decline is insignificant. The rise of input on the private economy is significant and positive.

Table 3.3: Sectoral Estimated Markups for the U.K Private Business Economy

No. Sectors	SIC 92	μ
2. Oil and Gas	11, 12	1.960
3. Coal & mining	10, 13, 14	1.004
4. Manufacturing fuel	23	1.144
5. Chemical & Pharmaceuticals	24	1.193
6. Non-metallic mineral products	26	1.199
7. Basic metals & metal goods	27, 28	1.148
8. Mechanical Engineering	29	0.934
9. Electrical Engineering & Electronics	30, 31, 32, 33	1.003
10. Vehicles	34, 35	1.147
11. Food, drink & tobacco	15, 16	0.989
12. Textiles, clothing & leather	17, 18, 19	1.074
13. Paper, printing & publishing	21, 22	1.148
14. Other manufacturing	20, 25, 36, 37	1.341
15. Electricity supply	40.1	1.296
16. Gas supply	40.2, 40.3	1.086
17. Water supply	41	1.154
18. Construction	45	1.237
19. Wholesale, vehicle sales & repairs	50, 51	1.477
20. Retailing	52	1.243
21. Hotels & catering	55	1.090
22. Rail transport	60.1	1.115
23. Road transport	60.2, 60.3	0.906
24. Water transport	61	0.850
25. Air transport	62	1.073
26. Other transport	63	0.793
27. Communications	64	0.954
28. Finance	65, 66	1.013
29. Business Services	67, 70, 71, 72, 73, 74	1.001
33. Waste treatment	90	1.223
34. Miscellaneous services	91 - 99	0.202

The table 3.3 shows the list of sectors that comprises of the U.K private business economy, their SIC classifications, including my estimations of the sectors markups that was used in the econometric modelling. The table 3.4 below is for the manufacturing sectors of the U.K economy only. The term μ denotes markup.

Table 3.4: U.K Manufacturing Sectors Markups (1970 – 2000)

No. Sectors	SIC 92	μ
Non-Durables		
4. Manufactured fuel	23	1.097
5. Chemical & pharmaceuticals	24	1.033
11. Food, drink & tobacco	15, 16	1.011
12. Textiles, clothing & leather	17, 18, 19	1.087
13. Paper, printing & publishing	21, 22	0.793
Durables		
6. Non-metallic mineral products	26	0.956
7. Basic metals & metal goods	27, 28	1.048
8. Mechanical engineering	29	0.942
9. Electrical engineering & electronics	30, 31, 32, 33	1.024
10. Vehicles	34, 35	0.951
14. Other manufacturing	20, 25, 36, 37	1.279

3.4   Conclusions

The aggregate technology used in this analysis has been obtained through the correction of the aggregate Solow residual (SR) for increasing returns, imperfect competition, and varying utilization of capital and labor. The results in table 3.2 show that, technology improvements do not contract input use overall.

Also very important in this study is the implication for monetary policy given the impact of technology shocks in the model. Monetary policy is crucial for the authorities to determine on how to react to technology shocks in order to adjust to the new level of full employment output. This is not withstanding the fact that monetary policy target is predominately for short run stabilization of the economy around moving target of full employment output. In other words, short run movements in technology growth are equally important as proper conduct of monetary policy as the long run rate of technology growth.

This study has provided a broad analysis of the impact of technology shocks, and employment / hours to enable policy and strategic decisions to be feasible. Finally, based on the evidence of the results so far, I cannot conclude yet on the impact of technology on hours, in other words, on the contractionary effects for the UK economy. In which case, I need to investigate further the disaggregate version of these regressions hence, forming the basis for chapters 4 and 5 of this thesis.

Notes & Discussions

Notes & Discussions

Chapter 4

Technology Shocks and Aggregate Fluctuations

4.1 Introduction

The theme of this chapter centres on the estimation of productivity and hours (or employment) including the decomposition into technology and non-technology shocks. The principal empirical methodology in this research follows the three competing strands of measurement approaches. The first of these approaches relates to the Gali (1999) methodology. Gali estimated a decomposition of productivity and hours into technology and non-technology components. The results from his study show the estimated conditional correlations of hour and productivity to be negative for technology shocks and positive for non-technology shocks. In addition, hours show a persistent decline in response to a positive technology shock. The evidence from Gali's study is difficult to reconcile with a conventional real business cycle interpretation of business cycles. However, it is consistent with a simple model with monopolistic competition and sticky prices.

The Real Business Cycle (RBC) models, made famous by the work of Kydland and Prescott (1982) and its subsequent extensions, explains the majority of aggregate fluctuations observed in the post-war U.S. economy as being consistent with the competitive equilibrium of a neoclassical growth model augmented with a labour-leisure choice and exogenous technology shocks. This has led to the proponents of the RBC paradigm claiming to its successful empirical performance as a reason for taking seriously its account of the mechanisms through which shocks affect the economy and propagated over time.

Thus, the Gali's method criticalness to the evidence supporting real business cycle (RBC) models predictions, especially on their ability to match the patterns of unconditional second moments of key macroeconomic time series. In addition, a number of studies support the Gali approach. For example, the study by Khan and Tsoukalas (2006) examined what happens after a neutral technology shock and reported that hours worked decline in a persistent manner in the UK. Their approach differs from this research methodology especially in the measurement of hours. Gali (1999) on the other hand, argued that in order to match some key second moments of the data, RBC economists must allow for multiple sources of fluctuations. Where this is the case, the model would yield predictions that are stronger than restrictions on the sign and/ or, pattern of unconditional second moments. Furthermore, it provided predictions in terms of conditional second moments, that is, second moments conditional on a given source of fluctuations. In that respect, an evaluation criterion based on the model's ability to match unconditional moments may be highly misleading. In other words, the model can perform well based on that criterion but at the same time present a highly distorted evidence of the economy's response to each type of shock. Thus, the demonstration in the context of a well-known anomaly associated with the RBC model, that is, its prediction of a high positive correlation between hours and labor productivity.

The other measurement approach I adopted relates to the BF (2002) and BFK (2004) as discussed in the previous chapter 3. BFK (2004) reported that hours declines on impact following technological improvements by using an augmented growth accounting method to identify technology shocks. I will therefore not discuss in detail their methodology in this chapter given its discussion in the previous chapters. The other studies of interest includes Shea (1998) using indicators of technological innovation identifies shocks to R & D and patent applications as a more direct measure of stochastic variations in technology. Shea postulation is that technology shocks raise short run labor input while decreasing it in the long run. The findings by these studies implies that technology shocks are not a significant source of economic fluctuations and as such do not provide support for the RBC predictions of business cycles. The reason presented to justify these findings is that models with nominal price stickiness creates a reduction in hours where monetary policy fails to make adequate provision for the technology shock (Khan et al (2006)).

The third approach is the Christiano, Eichenbaum and Vigfusson (CEV (2003)) method. This will essentially form our second or alternative approach to follow in this research. This methodology uses aggregate technology series, computed as in Basu, Fernald and Kimball (BFK (1999)) to show a rise in hours after technology shock. The motivation for this empirical research is precisely the interest to explore both sides of the arguments. In chapter one, I provided a comprehensive literature reviews of the various findings which reinforces these conclusions and their implications for evaluating business cycle theories. This is more so because of the number of contentious issues involved. The prominent ones among them extend to whether identified shocks represent variations in technology for example Francis and Ramey (2004) or the treatment of hours in the structural vector autoregression (SVAR) models such as in Christiano et al (2003). The other issues are the low frequency correlation between hours and productivity indicated by Fernald (2005) and CEV (2003).

There is in addition the issue of small sample biases and weakness of long run restrictions in identifying technology shocks since nontechnology shocks can have permanent impacts on labor productivity (Khan et al (2006), Faust and Leeper (1997), Uhlig (2004), Erceg et al (2005) and Christiano et al (2005)). Finally, the emerging issue is the debate about the role of investment specific versus neutral technology shocks as in Fisher (2005 and 2006). For further insight, one can refer to Gali and Rabanal (2004) who provided a comprehensive discussion and overview of the literature.

The prediction of RBC models focuses on the high positive correlation between hours and productivity. It assumes the source of the correlation is behind the mechanism propelling macro fluctuations in RBC models. More over, it implies a shift in the labor demand schedule caused by technology shocks together with an upward sloping labor supply. Thus, this empirical investigation of the two forms of models indicates their different implications regarding the responses of hours and productivity to each type of shock and therefore, their conditional correlations. Furthermore, Gali's stylized model provides an alternative perception to the productivity – hour's anomaly that deviates from the basic RBC paradigm[49].

The structure of this chapter is as follows: section 4.1 above gives the introduction, while section 4.2 discusses the first approach (Gali), while the specification and conditional correlation estimators form the discussion for section 4.2.1. The second approach (CEV) is in section 4.3. I provide in Section 4.4 a summary of the data used and testing approaches. In section 4.5, I discuss the empirical findings and results

---

[49] The stylized model uses a monopolistic competition, sticky prices and variable effort to explain the unconditional correlation between productivity and hours. Its prediction is that technology shocks generate a negative comovement between productivity and hours. However, the positive comovement arising from non-technology shocks then offset it (Gali, 1999, p.250 AER).

from the bivariate model, while section 4.6 is the 5-variable model. Section 4.7 is the conclusions.

4.2   The Model – First Approach (Gali, (1999))

I begin the exploration of the scope of this empirical study, by first employing the Gali stylised model of the analysis of labor market dynamics in a sticky price and variable labor efforts (the Keynesian Economics). The model approach involves taking a monetary model with a monopolistic competition, sticky prices and variable labor efforts. The hypothesis assumed that technology and monetary shocks are the two prime exogenous factors (see the appendix to chapter 4 for the technical analytical considerations).

The Empirical Framework

The empirical framework for the identification restriction process followed three assumptions. First is to assume that output is determined in line with a homogeneous of degree one, strictly concave, and aggregate production function given as:

$$Y_t = F(K_t, T_t, L_t) \tag{4.1}$$

Where Y_t is the output, K_t and L_t represent the effective capital and labor input services used respectively. By implementing the above equation, it allows for possible unobservable variations in the utilization rate of inputs, capital and labor. The term T_t represents an exogenous technology parameter following a stochastic process with a unit root. In other words, some technology shocks will have permanent effects on the level T_t. The second assumption is that the capital-labor ratio, which is a measure in efficiency units, $K_t / T_t L_t$ follows a stationary stochastic process. If r_t represents the return on physical capital, profit maximization will give the following expression:

$$r_t = \frac{F_k\left(\frac{K_t}{T_tL_t}, 1\right)}{mu} - d \qquad (4.2)$$

Where, mu denote mark-up and d is the depreciation rate. From equation (4.2), it implies that, with the assumption of stationarity of the markup including the depreciation rate, the capital-labor ratio will be stationary whenever the sequence of returns $\{r_t\}$ is stationary. Furthermore, this complies with RBC models that show fluctuations around a steady state as in Solow-Swan model or the Ramsey-Cass-Koopmans model.

Finally, the third assumption implies that, effective labor input L_t is a homogeneous of degree one function of hours N_t and efforts U_t, thus:

$$L_t = g(N_t, U_t) \qquad (4.3)$$

In addition, efforts per hour U_t / N_t will in this case follow a stationary stochastic process. The assumption is that homogeneity will be required if effective labor input is to be proportional to hours whenever effort per hour is constant. More over, stationarity of U_t / N_t is consistent with the existing RBC models with variable efforts (Gali, (1999) and Burnside et al (1993)).

Therefore, from equations (4.1) to (4.3), the expression for measured labor productivity is as $P_t = \frac{Y_t}{N_t} = \frac{Y_t}{L_t}\frac{L_t}{N_t} = T_t F\left(\frac{K_t}{T_tL_t}, 1\right)g\left(1, \frac{U_t}{N_t}\right)$. In log form, the expression is as:

$$p_t = t_t + \xi_t \qquad (4.4)$$

Under the three assumptions mentioned, $\xi_t \equiv \log F\left(K_t / T_tL_t, 1\right)g\left(1, U_t / N_t\right)$ and stationary, hence, making equation (4.4) crucial for the identification of technology shocks. The most important thing with this identification process centres on the understanding that only the permanent changes in the stochastic component of technology parameter t_t can be the source of the unit root in productivity. In other words, it assumes only technology shocks can have a permanent effect on the level of labor productivity. Equally, it is important to note there may be other possible sources of shocks in the economy that can affect labor productivity through its impacts on effort per hour and the capital-labor ratio, for example, government purchases or monetary shocks.

The empirical framework thus, establishes the decomposition of hours and productivity in line with technology and nontechnology shocks as in Gali (1999). Therefore, by using the structural vector autoregressive (SVAR) model, I can estimate the conditional comovements. In addition, it enables equation (4.4) to identify the restriction that only technology shocks might possess a permanent effect on the level of productivity as well as complying with RBC models and/or models with nominal rigidities.

The computation of the conditional correlations of hours and productivity variations came from the impulse response coefficients of the structural moving average (MA) representation. An example can be found in, Gali (1996), Baxter and King (1993), Shapiro and Watson (1988), and Blanchard and Summers (1986). The approach does not require the usual assumptions necessary to construct Solow residual based measures of technology shocks, such as, time varying markups, capital utilization and corrections for labor hoarding. For the effects of markup in the business cycle, Banerjee and Russell (2000) and (2002); and Banerjee, Cockerell and Russell (2001) provided very good examples. In terms of the drawbacks with the model as hypothesizes by Gali, it may probably not adequately satisfy the requirements for an endogenous growth model, where all shocks affect productivity in the long run, as well as in standard model when there are permanent shocks to the tax rate on capital income.

4.2.1   The Specification and Conditional Correlation Estimators

We specify the adopted Gali approach, by assuming the observed variations in (log) productivity (p_t), that is $p_t = \ln\left(\frac{Y}{L}\right)$ and log hours (n_t) to originate from two exogenous disturbances namely technology and non-technology shocks. These are orthogonal to each other and their impact propagates over time through unspecified mechanisms. The model also assumes that the vector $[\Delta p_t, \Delta n_t]$ is an expression of a possible infinite distributed lag of technology and non-technology shocks. Thus the expression in a matrix form as

$$\begin{bmatrix} \Delta p_t \\ \Delta n_t \end{bmatrix} = \begin{bmatrix} C^{11}(L)C^{12}(L) \\ C^{21}(L)C^{22}(L) \end{bmatrix} \begin{bmatrix} \varepsilon_t^z \\ \varepsilon_t^m \end{bmatrix} \equiv C(L)\varepsilon_t \tag{4.5}$$

Where, $\{\varepsilon_t^z\}$ and $\{\varepsilon_t^m\}$ represents technology and non-technology shocks. The orthogonality assumption with a standard normalization, indicate $E\varepsilon_t\varepsilon_t' = 1$. The identifying restriction for the unit root of productivity originates exclusively from technology shocks relation to $C^{12}(1) = 0$. Hence, the matrix of long run multipliers C (1) is constrained to the lower triangular. In addition, C (1) is the cumulated effects of $C^{11}(L)$ In equation (4.5), the integration of both productivity and hours are of the order one. This means that it may be necessary to difference the variables to achieve stationarity.

I show the results in tables 4.1 and 4.2. In addition, equation (4.5) also contains the consistent estimates of the coefficients of C (L) as a function of the estimated parameters of a reduced-form VAR for $[\Delta p_t, \Delta n_t]$. The estimate for C (L) is set firmly in the impulse response coefficients. Having set the parameters for the reduced form VAR, I therefore, establish imposed restrictions, hence, the expression for the estimate of conditional correlations as:

$$\rho\left(\Delta p_t, \Delta n_t / i\right) = \frac{\sum_{j=0}^{\infty} C_j^{1i} C_j^{2i}}{\sqrt{\text{var}\left(\Delta p_t / i\right) \text{var}\left(\Delta n_t / i\right)}} \tag{4.6}$$

Where, $i = z, m$ while, $\text{var}(\Delta p_t / i) = \sum_{j=0}^{\infty} (C_j^{1i})$ and $\text{var}(\Delta n_t / i) = \sum_{j=0}^{\infty} (C_j^{2i})$ are conditional variances of productivity growth and hours growth. This will eventually tend to infinite. With respect to stationarity, I therefore performed robust diagnostic checks including standard procedures, of the ADF unit root test. The checks or tests also helped to determine choice of variables to utilise in the estimations.

4.3   The Alternative Methodological Approach

In this section, I explain the Christiano, Eichenbaum and Vigfusson ((CEV) (2004) methodological approach. The distinction between the CEV and the Gali model discussed above centres on the identification assumptions. The previous approach indirectly assumed innovation to technology is the only shock that have a long run impact on labour productivity. A number of RBC models of course support this (Christiano (1988), King et al (1991), Christiano and Eichenbaum (1992)).

Similarly, BFK (1999) and (2004) on the other hand estimated an innovation to technology through direct measure of technology[50]. The method involves measuring aggregate technology based on industry level data. It does not assume technology shocks are the only shocks with permanent impact on labor productivity. Equally, BFK find hours worked fall after a positive technology shock, whereas in the Gali (1999) approach hours also fall following positive technology shocks, identified as permanent shocks to labor productivity through long run restrictions in a structural vector autogression (SVAR). Since the advent of the seminal paper by Kydland and Prescott (1982), RBC theory has developed by emphasizing shocks to technology as drivers of economic

---

[50] This is a formulation from the Solow-residual accounting. Other examples include Burnside, Eichenbaum and Rebelo (1995), Burnside and Eichenbaum (1996) – on Solow residual based measures of technology correcting for labour hoarding and capacity utilizations.

fluctuations with a prediction of increase in output and hours worked after positive technology shocks.

The CEV approach therefore, is an application of an encompassing method of assessing the plausibility of the conflicts emanating from the Gali and BFK, and the RBC conclusions on hours rise and/or fall after a positive technology shock. CEV finding is that based on long run identifying assumptions, hours worked rise in response to a positive technology shock. Therefore, the intention in this section is to use similar methods to see if the findings hold. The debate about the long run identification using labour productivity advances contradictory conclusions in relation to hours worked rising or falling after technology shock. This is because the inference is sensitive to modelling details. For instance, by quadratically detrending or first differencing logarithm, per capita hours worked leads to assumption that hour's fall after a positive technology shock.

An example to the above views relates to the treatment of the low frequency components of hours worked. Thus, by quadratically detrending all variables or modelling per capita hours as stationary in levels can lead to conclusion that hours rise. Hence, CEV (2004) applied an encompassing approach to assess the relative plausibility of these conflicting conclusions. They find that, on balance, the evidence based on long run identifying assumptions favours the view that hours worked rise in response to a positive technology shock. Now, contrasting this with the BFK, where they developed a measure of aggregate technology based on industry-level data, with a conclusion that hours worked fall after a positive technology shock. This means that, there is a conflict between the conclusions reached in BFK and those of CEV. Furthermore, as postulated by CEV, the BFK approach contains two fundamental assumptions namely; the measure of technology that is exogenous and hours worked which is difference stationary. Hence, CEV disagree with the assumptions and hence replaces them with an alternative which leads to hours worked rising after a positive technology shock. Hence, the conclusion that the approach based on long run identification with labour productivity and the one based on direct measures of technology shocks does give similar conclusions. A simple explanation for this is that, the BFK exogeneity assumption means the one-step-ahead innovation in their measure of technology complies with the innovation to true technology.

Therefore, technology is not Granger-caused by other variables. This is assuming that agents do not observe or react to advance signals on the innovation to technology. If on the other hand, agents observe or react to it, then the variables that react to advance signals will Granger-cause true technology. More over if the level of hours worked helps forecast the growth rate of technology, while true technology is exogenous, the BFK measure of technology is perplex by measurement error. This is because of the existence of measurement error induces Granger-causality.

The problem here is that similar assumption can also apply to forecast errors in technology. The measurement errors in this case would apply to discrepancies between true and measured outputs and inputs due to the economy adjustments method to shocks. For instance, labor hoarding, capacity utilization and cyclical movements in the markup. For example, Banerjee and Russell (2002) indicate that the markup on marginal costs is counter-cyclical and thus, the re-interpretation as a short run relationship between changes in the markup and the business cycle. Their finding identifies the source of the cyclical variation in the markup on unit costs as due to the counter-cyclical behavior of the change in productivity and not because of any cyclical behavior of the change in the markup of price on average wages.

One possible technique to counteract the measurement errors if that is the case could be to use Vigfusson (2002) strategy for handling measurement error. This would involve replacing the assumption that measured technology is exogenous with the assumption that, true innovations to technology are the only shock that affects BFK's measure of technology. Therefore, the assumption of transient distortions in the long run to the BFK technology series will allow for the adoption of Gali (1999) long run identification method to recover estimates of the shocks to technology from BFK's measure of technology.

In terms of the Granger-causality the assumption is that, there is a sizeable endogenous component to technology. In this case, all economic shocks have an impact on technology. Further more, in reference to BFK's additional assumption that hours worked are difference stationary, CEV finds evidence against the assumption, including the hypothesis that per capita hours worked is difference stationary. The CEV view is that there should be no first differencing of per capita hours based on evidence from encompassing argument. Hence, CEV application of long run identification to the BFK measure of technology and utilizing the level of hours worked finds innovation to technology leading to a rise in hours worked.

In Khan et al (2006), they identify technology shocks, by adopting two types of restrictions. First is the imposition of long run restriction, requiring the unit root in labor productivity to be exclusively driven by technology shocks as in Gali (1999). The second approach imposes medium run restriction as proposed by Uhlig (2004). This procedure identifies the most persistent shock to labor productivity over a three to ten year horizon without imposing a unit root. The reason for this identification is the concern that shocks other than technology such as capital income tax, might have a permanent impact on labor productivity. Where this applies, the presumption is that it would invalidate the identifying assumption under long run restrictions. Hence, Uhlig (2004) utilises stimulated data from dynamic general equilibrium model (DGEM) to indicate medium run restrictions are more robust relative to long run restrictions in identifying technology shocks. Furthermore, Faust and Leeper (1997) in assessing the long run restrictions, imply that the distinction between a very persistent and a unit root process in finite data is probably unpronounced leading to less reliable identification.

For the alternative approach, I used total actual hours worked and measured technology series for the period 1971:1 – 2006:4. For the steps in the estimation of the BFK TFP see chapters two and three, which are for the period 1970 - 2000. I converted the hours worked to per capita by dividing it with a measure of the population. For similar use of per capita, see Francis and Ramey (2001), Mulligan (2002) and CEV (2003).

4.3.1 Explanation of the VAR Model

In this chapter 4 and in chapter 5 next, Structural Vector Autoregressive (SVAR) model played a major role in our empirical expositions. Sims (1980) proposed a model with a dynamic specification to use to test causal linkages rather than imposing them. The alternative advocated is the vector autoregressive or VAR model. The VAR model is a multiple variable generalisation of the autoregressive model. The regressors are lags of all the variables in the model. Since there are no current endogenous variables on the right-hand side of the equations, there is no need imposing restrictions to identify the system. The set of regressors are the same for each equation so that each equation is estimated efficiently using the OLS estimator. The VAR model in this case ignores economic restrictions, hence, assuming it as 'a theoretic'. It also regards it as a reduced form of simultaneous equations system where the predetermined variables are all lagged dependent variables and there are no pure exogenous variables.

Specifying the empirical VAR to correspond with the theory involves two elements of arbitrariness. First, the economic theory does not normally provide indications regarding the lag length of VAR models. Therefore, two approaches can be taken in this case, either a prior choose lag length and verify that the results are independent of this auxiliary assumption or to let the data choose the correct lag length using optimal statistical criteria such as Akaike (1974) or Schwartz (1978).

Secondly, many dynamic models tend to deliver solutions for the vector of endogenous variables with covariance matrix being singular because there are large numbers of endogenous variables than shocks. In which case, to undertake a meaningful estimation, it is essential to complete the model by adding other sources of disturbances. For example, one possible source for this new disturbance could be a measurement error. In other words, there could be an induce Granger-causality.

The concept of Granger causality starts with the premise that the future cannot cause the past. If event A occurs after event B, then A cannot cause B. Granger (1969), applies this concept to economic time series to determine whether one time series causes in the sense that precedes another. However, merely because event A occurs before B does not mean that A causes B. For example, New Year shopping does not cause New Year. Granger causality relates to the question of how useful one variable or set of variables y_1 is for forecasting another variable or set of variables x_1.

If on the other hand, y_1 does not Granger cause x_1 then y_1 does not help to forecast x_1. For example, if Y does not cause X in Granger's definition if, and only if, in the moving average representation:

$$\begin{bmatrix} X(t) \\ Y(t) \end{bmatrix} = \begin{bmatrix} a.....b \\ c.....d \end{bmatrix} * \begin{bmatrix} u \\ v \end{bmatrix}(t)$$

a or b can be chosen to be identically zero, $v(t)$ is orthogonal to $u(t)$, that is, the residual in a regression. Both $v(t)$ and $u(t)$ are uncorrelated with past values of each other. In addition, $v(t)$ and $u(t)$ are contemporaneously uncorrelated. Equally, when $\begin{bmatrix} X \\ Y \end{bmatrix}$ has an autoregressive representation, Y can be expressed as a distributed lag function of current and past X with a residual which is not correlated with any X(s), past or future if, and only if, Y does not cause X in Granger sense (Sims 1972).

The measurement error in this case would refer to transient, high frequency discrepancies between true and measured outputs and inputs that occur because of the way the economy adjusts to shocks. It could also be from labour hoarding, capacity utilization and/or from cyclical movements in the mark-up. These issues we have touched on earlier in the previous sections of this chapter. Therefore, without any further ado, the usual assumption is that agents will have an information set that is larger than the one in use[51]. Thus, the estimated VAR is non-singular because of omission of important sources of dynamics from the model. Furthermore, the assumption is ε_t^z is the first element of e_t. Therefore, by regressing u_t on ε_t^z by the VAR disturbances gives the computation of the dynamic response of the variables in Y_t to ε_t^z as the first column of C.

4.4 Data Analysis and Hours Stationarity Test

The measurement of hours per capita is an important part of many studies as indicated by Francis and Ramey (2004). The Real Business Cycle model analysis usually compares predictions from the model to the behaviour of hours per capita in the data. Equally, the effect of technology shocks on hours is evident that different maintained assumptions concerning the stationarity of hours per capita can lead to different outcomes. This has led to many studies measuring hours per capita as total hours worked in the private sector divided by the civilian non-institutional population aged 16 and over.

---

[51] See for example, Christiano & Eichenbaum (1992), "liquidity effects, monetary policy and the business cycle". NBER working paper no. 1429.

The data I used in this study for labor input are official seasonally adjusted time series. Hence, it can be expected for positive technology shock, identified through long-run restriction to be capable of leading to a decrease in hours irrespective of assumptions that hours per capita are stationary or non-stationary. For example in figures 4.1a & b below, per capita hours exhibit a stationarity trend. I therefore, examine carefully the definitions of hours worked employed in the estimations. In this respect, I defined hours worked in four different ways, namely:

CBH: total hours worked divided by the total workforce.

CBPH: total hours worked divided by a measure of the civilian population.

CPH: Average total hours per week worked divided by the civilian population.

CPHRS: Average hours worked divided by the workforce.

4.4.1   Data and Variables Definitions

BEHRS	Bank of England Industry Dataset Hours (annual)
CBH	BEHRS / Total Workforce
CBPH	BEHRS / Civilian Population
CPH	Average Hours (AVHRS) / Civilian Population
CPHRS	AVHRS / Total Workforce
LBH	Log of BEHRS
ΔBH	First difference of LBH
BHPFCYC	HP Filter of LBH
LBHT	Detrended LBH
LAH	Log of AVHRS
AHT	log of AVHRS detrended
ΔAH	First difference of LAH

CPOP	Measure of civilian population
LCBH	Log of CBH
ΔCBH	First difference of LCBH
LCBPH	Log of CBPH
$\Delta CBPH$	First difference of LCBPH
LCPH	Log of CPH
ΔCPH	First difference of LCPH
LCPHRS	Log of CPHRS
$\Delta CPHRS$	First difference of LCPHRS
HPF	Hodrick-Prescott Filter
HPCYC	Cycle series (Lah.hpf (100) hptrend01 i.e., HPF (Lambda = 100)
Δt_hrs	BFK estimation technology (productivity) after hour's utilization
PCH	AVHRS / Total Workforce
LPCH	Log of PCH
ΔPCH	First difference of LPCH

Note: All variables beginning with the letter (Δ) are in first difference and all with (L) are in log levels. AVHRS (average hours) is a measure of total actual weekly hours worked in millions. The measure of civilian population is population less HM Forces and Government Employees.

As shown in figures 4.1a and figure 4.1b below, it does not matter which hours is used, it will still yield the same result. The UK hour's data used are trending downwards while US hours for the Gali study is not trending. In addition, the US hours are not stationary but the UK hours are trend stationary and robust. The trend and cyclicality of the four different definitions are of the same pattern.

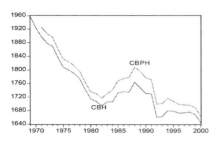 

Figure 4.1a UK: Stationarity - hours

Figure 4.1b Stationarity- hours

In addition, I then derive the total hours worked by averaging over the 4 quarters. The hour week is quarterly hours divide by total employees (of 16 years and above), this then give the per capita hours. The data sources are from the UK office of national statistics, the labor force surveys (ONS-LFS), the Bank of England Industry Dataset (BEID), the OECD, the IMF IFS and the World Bank. The ONS-LFS dataset used is for the period 1970:1 – 2006:4. Figure 4.1c below shows the trend of the UK hours using the ONS data.

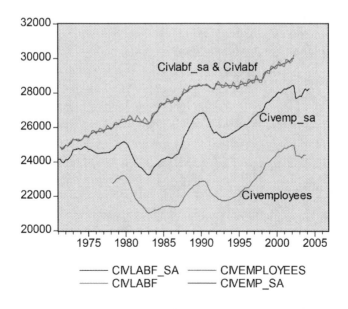

Figure 4.1C: The Different Hours Series

This relies on estimates of structural VAR for labor input and productivity measures using UK quarterly data for the period 1970:Q1 – 2006:Q4. The two alternative labor input series are the log of employed civilian labor force denoted as n_e and the Log of total employee hours represented as n_h. Equally, the representation for the two alternative time series for log productivity are P_e and P_h respectively. The constructions are as the difference between log (GDP) that is, y and the corresponding labor input measures n_e and P_e (log of employed civilian labor force and productivity). The other forms are n_h and P_h (total employee hours worked). Therefore, productivity is $(\lg dp - n_e)$ and $(\lg dp - n_h)$. I also carried out a Hodrick-Prescott Filter (HPF) estimation that applies to each component of employment and productivity. I also detrended the variables as well as taking first differences. In the estimations, I made use of the first differences variables since they yield the same results as the detrended ones.

4.4.2   Variables definition - Bivariate model

CES	:	Civilian employees
LCES	:	Log of (CES)
$\Delta LCES$	:	First difference of (LCES)
LCES_HPF	:	Hodrick-Prescott Filter series of LCES
LCES_det	:	Detrended (LCES)
TEH	:	Employee total
LTEH	:	Log (TEH)
Lteh_det	:	Detrended (LTEH) (Employment hours)
Δh_i	:	First difference (LTEH)
LY	:	Log of (y) (Productivity – using (TEH))
ΔY	:	First difference of (LY)
HPY	:	HPF series of (LY)
LCY	:	Log of Productivity series - (using LCES)
ΔCY	:	First difference of (LCY)
HPCY	:	HPF series of LCY

The definition for Labor is the total employee hours worked. Productivity is the GDP less total employees. The data for some quarters were missing in the CES series. The calculation for obtaining the missing data is by averaging the preceding previous four quarters. The unit root ADF test including HPF estimation is for all the complete data series.

Diagnostic Test: Robustness Check

Unit Root (UR) Test on $(\Delta M 0)$

In table, 4.1 are the results of the diagnostic tests. The Kwiatkowski-Phillips-Schmidt-Shin (KPSS) UR test (1992, Table 1) is 0.49 and significant at 5 percent asymptotic critical values. In accordance with the null hypothesis, $(\Delta M 0)$ is stationary. The estimation has a bandwidth of 7 (Newey-West using Bartlett kernel). The Elliot-Rothenberg-Stock (ERS) (1996, table 1) Point-Optimal Unit Root Test on $(\Delta M 0)$ is 7.07 and significant at 10 percent. Also with a constant and lag length of 2 (spectral OLS AR based on SIC) and includes 119 observations after adjustments. The Ng-Perron (Ng-P) Modified Unit Root Tests on $(\Delta M 0)$ also has a UR with lag length of 2 (spectral GLS-Detrended AR based on SIC). The test shows (MSB) $(0.35***)$ and (MPT) $(6.62***)$, both significant at 10 percent asymptotic critical values. The (MZa), and (MZt) were not significant. Asterisk denotes the asymptotic critical values, (*) – 1%, (**) – 5% and (***) at 10% respectively. The KPSS, Ng-Perron and ERS tests provide improvements over the ADF test. The purpose for our assumption of UR as the null hypothesis (that is, stationarity) is for confirmatory analysis together with the ADF test. In other words, it confirms the conclusion about the unit roots and if it rejects the null, then we do not have a confirmation.

The reason for these tests is the problem of size distortion and low power of the UR tests. The distribution of the Dickey-Fuller (DF) test is significantly different from the reported DF if the underlying distribution contains a moving-average (MA) component. Further more, the Phillips-Perron (PP) (1988) test suffers from size distortions when the MA parameter is large, which is usually the case with many economic time series (Schwert (1989)). Thus, the use of Ng- Perron (Ng-P) modified test in this case. Equally, DeJong et al (1992a) observed that the UR tests have low power against plausible trend-stationary alternatives. The ADF test displays size distortions in the presence of negatively correlated MA errors and the PP for plausibly correlated MA or AR error structures, hence the need for tests with higher power (Agiakoglou and Newbold (1992)).

Unit Root Test $(\Delta M4)$

Data source: ONS_LFS Sample (adjusted) 1971:Q1 – 2000:Q4. The term $(\Delta M0)$ denotes the growth in M0. The UR test in all the estimations in table 4.1 includes a constant with a lag length of 2, automatic based on SIC, except for the KPSS. The Augmented Dickey Fuller (ADF) unit root test is 3.65 and significant at 1 percent test critical values. The Mackinnon (1996) is a one-sided p-value of 0.00 and significant at 1 percent.

Table 4.1: Unit Root Test on ($\Delta M 0$)

Estimations	t-Stat		P-values	LM-Stat
ADF	-3.65*		0.00	
KPSS				0.49**
ERS			7.07***	
	MZa	**MZt**	**MSB**	**MPT**
Ng-P	-3.72	-1.30	0.35***	6.62***

Unit Root Test on ($\Delta M 4$)

Estimations	t-Stat	P-values	LM-Stat
ADF	-2.64***	0.08*	
KPSS			0.81*
ERS		3.95**	

Unit Root Test on ($\Delta M 4R$)

ADF	-6.20*	0.00*	
KPSS			0.17***
ERS		0.51	

Unit Root Test on (ΔP)

ADF	-2.70***	0.07*	
KPSS			1.07*
ERS		1.81	

Unit Root Test on LH

ADF	-2.89**	0.04*	
KPSS			0.46**

LH: Constant & Linear Trend

ADF	-3.35**	0.06*	
KPSS			0.20**

LH CE: Constant & Linear Trend (1971Q3 – 2004Q2)

ADF	-2.85	0.18*

LH CL : Constant, Linear Trend (1972 :Q1 – 2002 :Q2)

ADF	-2.44	0.35*

RR : Constant (1971Q2-2006Q4)

ADF	-2.73***	0.07*	
ERS		2.17*	
KPSS			0.47**

Data source: ONS_LFS Sample (adjusted) 1971:Q1 – 2006:Q4 otherwise specified.

The term ($\Delta M 4$) is the growth in M4. Sample (adjusted) 1971:Q2 – 2006:Q4. The estimation for the ADF test includes a constant, with a lag length of 4 which is automatic based on SIC. The growth of M4 has a unit root of -2.64 with a test critical value of 10 percent and p-values of 0.08*. The KPSS test is stationary with LM-Stat of 0.81* and significant at one percent asymptotic critical values. The bandwidth is 9 plus a constant. The ERS has a unit root of 3.95**, significant at 5 percent plus a constant and lag length of 4. It includes observations of 143 after adjustments. The other diagnostic tests are contained in table 4.1 above.

All estimations are separate regressions. LH = log of Hours. LH_CE = Log of Hours of civilian employees. LH_CL = Log of Hours of civilian labor force. RR = Real interest rate. The rest of the variables are in first difference or growth rates. The ADF tests for the log level variables stationarity are inconclusive, despite the detection of a unit root. The tests for the real interest rates (RR) have a unit root and stationary in KPSS test. All the tests results in table 4.1 are robust and justify our use of the variables.

4.5   The Empirical Findings and Results

I commence in this section by considering the conditional productivity-labor input co-movements and then proceeds to show some evidence based on the bivariate model estimates. The bivariate modelling is important because in most applied disciplines the real observable facts are usually multi-dimensional. The implication of this is that, there is more than one quantifiable feature for consideration[52]. The bivariate model results in table 4.2 are from the estimated equation (4.5) using the U.K quarterly data for the period 1971:1 to 2006:4. The baseline series for labor-input is the log of total employee- hours (seasonal adjusted)[53] denoting "hours" and the ONS labors statistics.

---

[52] See for example, Aris Spanos (1986), Statistical Foundation of Econometric Modelling. Chapter 3, p.85, Cambridge University Press

[53] Data for U.K obtained from the OECD.

Table 4.2: Bivariate Estimations (SVAR): Correlations

Estimates	Unconditional $cor(\Delta t, \Delta n)$	Conditional on: Technology $cor(\Delta t, \Delta n / \varepsilon^{z})$	Nontechnology $cor(\Delta t, \Delta n / \varepsilon^{m})$
$\Delta p_t, \hat{n}_t$ (total hours)	-0.23	-0.55	-0.07
	(-3.14)**	(-5.01)**	(-0.74)
$\Delta p_t, \Delta n_t$ First diff	0.33	0.39	0.27
	(3.69)**	(1.02)	(1.98)**
$\Delta p_t, \hat{n}_t$ (CE)	-0.01	-0.97	0.44
	(-0.12)	(-3.01)**	(3.34)**
$\Delta p_t, \Delta n_t$ (CE)	-0.48	-0.49	-0.47
	(-5.27)**	(-1.32)	(-2.90)**
$\Delta p_t, \hat{n}_t$ (CLF)	-0.04	-0.70	-0.60
	(-0.49)	(-0.92)	(-0.99)
$\Delta p_t, \Delta n_t$ (CLF)	-0.31	-0.12	-0.54
	(-3.57)**	(-0.33)	(-2.66)**

Data source: ONS-LFS. All estimations are separate regressions. The variable $\hat{n}_t$ denotes deviations of log hours from a fitted linear time trend. This is then used in the regressions. The term CE = Hours Civilian Employees. CLF = Hours Civilian Labour force. All regressions are shown on first differenced respectively. The asterisks (**) denotes significance at 5% critical value level. The standard errors are shown in parentheses. Table 4.2 is the estimates of unconditional and conditional correlations between the levels and growth of productivity and labour input (hours or employment) in the UK using quarterly data.

The result shows an evidence of contractionary effect for the UK economy. In row 1 of table 4.4, it implies the unconditional total hours worked declined by 23 percent. With the imposition of long run restriction, the decline arising due to technology is 55 percent and significant at 5 percent critical level, while that of nontechnology is 7 percent and insignificant. This means that most of the shocks are due to technology improvements affecting hours. First differencing total hours worked, the effect is a positive outcome and this is in row 2 of table 4.2. All the other results in that table gave negative correlation between labor productivity and hours both on the level and growth rates estimations.

Therefore, given the representations, one would be inclined to concur with Gali's model that the short-term rigidities in aggregate demand could be due to the stickiness of the price level and as the negative co-movement between productivity and employment (hours) after a technology shock as also shown in figure 4.2 below. However, in the long-term there seems to be a positive comovement generated by demand as in figure 4.3.

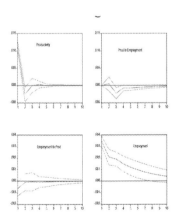

Figure 4.2: Productivity and Employment

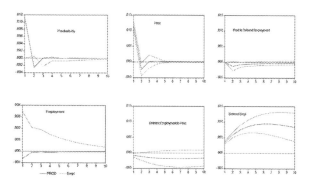

Figure 4.3: Impulse Responses Bivariate Model – de-trended hours

The unobserved effort variations can also explain the positive co-movement induced by demand shocks. The figure 4.2 shows the estimated impulse responses based on the model with first difference. In response to a positive technology shock of size equal to Cholesky one-standard deviation, labor productivity indicates an instant increase of about 0.4 percent and subsequently stabilising at a level higher. Output also experiences a permanent increase but more gradual than productivity for the detrended LBHT. The gap between the initial rise in labor productivity and output manifests by a short-term persistent decline in hours.

The negative conditional correlations found in the results are due to the joint variations in employment and productivity coming from technology shock taking place on impact. Under such circumstance, the variables drift into opposite directions as shown in figures 4.2 and 4.3. As for the positive correlation from the estimated dynamic responses to a non-technology shock, it shows a persistent positive effect on hours and productivity. The impact on hours and output can therefore, account for the source of the unit root detected in hours. Equally, the positive co-movement of productivity and hours on impact is responsible for the positive sign in the estimated correlation conditional on non-technology shocks. There is also retention of some of the qualitative patterns in the impulse responses when de-trended hours are used. De-trend are obtained from the deviations of log hours from a fitted line time trend as shown in figure 4.3 above.

Appropriateness of the definitions

In terms of the appropriateness of the definitions of hours used in table 4.2, the result shows that $\Delta p_t, \Delta n_t$ (first differenced hours) estimation is the most preferred. Its expansionary effect is consistent with the RBC models, while others are not. Under the log level hours, it yields a negative impact or contraction. In addition, the result between the two implies that, the main intuition therefore is not about the methodological approach, but essentially one of empirical argument. The empirical implication is because hours used in logarithmic levels are trending and therefore requires detrending to achieve stationarity (see figure 4.1a and 4.1b) and note on figure 4.2. Equally, hours in this model gives a better response following a positive technology shocks in capturing the dynamic effects in the economy. This is because increases in observed inputs (total hours or hours per worker) can be a proxy for unobserved changes in utilisation such as capacity utilization and labor effort.

The designing of the estimations in table 4.2 takes into consideration the various important debates in the recent literatures, see for example, literatures summary in chapter 1 of this book. This relates to the measures of labor input, stationarity assumptions, identification schemes and VAR specifications. It implies that, given the evidence of decline in hours it is therefore favorable for models with nominal price stickiness, low substitutability between domestic and foreign consumption, and investment specific shocks.

4.6   The Evidence from a Five-Variable Model

In this section, the objective is to determine the robustness of the estimates. Hence, in furtherance to the models approach, I estimated a higher dimensional (five-variable) VAR model. This allows for four orthogonal non-technology shocks. The data used in the specification of the model include data on money, interest rates, prices, productivity and labour-input series used in the bivariate model (see the diagnostic test table and the appendix to this chapter for further evidence). I denote the measure of the stock of money for the five variable models by m. The estimation uses the real growth in M4 instead of M0. The reason is that M4 has a longer series than M0. In any case, the choice of variable did not affect the results. The price measure P_x is the log of the consumer price index CPI. The nominal interest rate r is the three-month Treasury Bills. In the estimation, both the real interest rate and the inflation rate entered in levels. They were not first difference simply because there are no theoretical requirements to do so.

Table 4.3: Five-Variable Model: Estimates

5-Var Estimation	Unconditional	Conditional on: Technology Nontechnology	
$(\Delta p_t \ n_t \ \Delta m_t \ rr_t \ \Delta \pi_t)$ (log level hours)	0.02 (1.08)	0.01 (0.78)	0.02 (0.16)
$(\Delta p_t \ \Delta n_t \ \Delta m_t \ rr_t \ \Delta \pi_t)$ (First-difference hours)	0.16 (2.56)**	-0.02 (-0.28)	0.31 (1.46)
$(\Delta p_t \ \Delta n_t \_ce \ \Delta m_t \ rr_t \ \Delta \pi_t)$	0.47 (6.31)**	0.58 (7.85)**	-0.26 (-4.59)**
$(\Delta p_t \ \Delta n_t \_ce \ \Delta m_t \ rr_t \ \Delta \pi_t)$	0.44 (5.47)**	0.56 (6.96)**	-0.60 (-9.53)**
$(\Delta p_t \ \Delta n_t \_cl \ \Delta m_t \ rr_t \ \Delta \pi_t)$	-0.04 (-1.19)	-0.02 (-0.56)	-0.05 (-0.32)
$(\Delta p_t \ \Delta emp_t \_ce \ \Delta m_t \ rr_t \ \Delta \pi_t)$	0.28 (2.15)**	-0.13 (-0.39)	0.59 (3.68)**
$(\Delta p_t \ \Delta emp_t \_cl \ \Delta m_t \ rr_t \ \Delta \pi_t)$	0.36 (3.53)**	0.43 (1.07)	0.46 (1.87)*

Table 4.6: shows the results from the five variable models estimations – unconditional estimation and a decomposed technology estimation (technology and non-technology estimates).

4.6.1   Results

Table 4.1 shows the unit root test while table 4.2 is the conditional correlation estimates for the BSVAR and table 4.3 the five variable or higher dimension model. The results from the unit root test are for the series I used in the five variables model are in table 4.4. The tests fail to reject the null hypothesis of a unit root in the levels of all the series at 5% tests critical values as indicated in the tables.

For the first difference, it systematically rejected the null. These results imply a characterization of $\{[p_t, n_t]'\}$ as I (1) process. It therefore supports the benchmark VAR specification used. In addition, it does not make much difference if hours or employment is used. The results of the unit root tests used in the five-variable VAR are consistent with the hypothesis of a unit root in the nominal rate (r_t), the growth rate of the money supply (Δm_t), and inflation $(\Delta \pi_t)$. The tests do not reject the null that money growth (Δm) and inflation $(\Delta \pi)$ are co-integrated with co-integrating vector [1, -1], implying a stationary process for the rate of growth of real balances at 10% level $\{\Delta m_t - \Delta \pi_t\}$. For the nominal rate (r_t) and inflation $(\Delta \pi_t)$ the same properties hold, implying a stationary (ex-post) real interest rate process $\{r - \Delta \pi_{t+1}\}$ or (rr_t). This means that the three variables have a single common trend[54].

4.6.2   Additional Analysis

I show here the ADF Unit Root tests in table 4.4. Therefore, using our different definitions of hours worked, the graphs in figures 4.4 to 4.6 are from the data constructed.

Table 4.4: The Augmented Dickey-Fuller (ADF) Unit Root ADF Test

Variables	Level		First Difference	
	t-stats	P-values	t-stats	P-values
CBH	-2.39	0.3728	-4.56*	0.0053
CBPH	-2.00	0.5751	-3.91**	0.0250
CPH	-3.37***	0.0756	-4.15**	0.0146
CPHRS	-3.04	0.1389	-4.25**	0.0117
Δt_hours	-6.81*	0.0001	-3.12	0.1265
ΔP_x	-3.29***	0.0864	-5.69*	0.0004
HPCYC	-4.53*	0.0061	-4.37*	0.0092

Sources: ONS-LFS and BEID Annual series (1970 – 2000). Test Critical Values: 1% level = -4.28, 5% = -3.56 and 10% = -3.21. *Mackinnon (1996) One-Sided p-values.

---

[54] This is consistent with studies by Shapiro and Watson (1988), and Gali (1992).

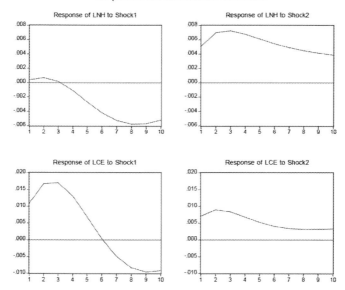

Figure 4.4

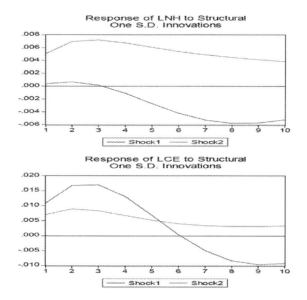

Figure 4.5

Figure 4.4 - 4.6: Impulse responses to level specification: Bivariate hours

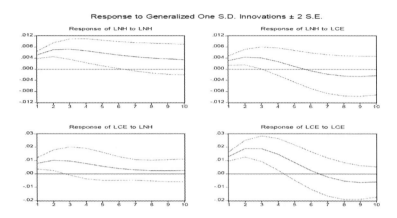

Figure 4.6

The figures 4.4 – 4.6 are the impulse responses functions corresponding to the level specification indicating the basic qualitative results from the bivariate analysis on hours and employment to shocks. Both variables rise in hump-shape patterns after a positive shock to technology. The contemporaneous effect of the shock is to drive output and hours up, while the long run effect is to raise hours and output. The graphs below show the impulse responses for the two levels.

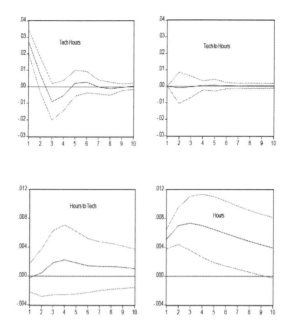

Figure 4.7: Multiple graphs (log level)

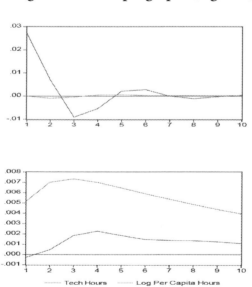

Figure 4.8: Combined graph

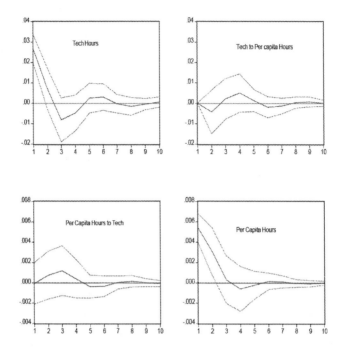

Figure 4.9: First difference level

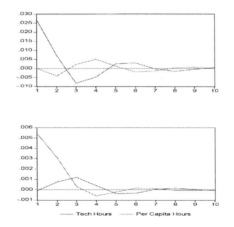

Figure 4.10 Combined Response Graph

Figure 4.7 – 4.10 is Cholesky S.D based on the impulse response of SVAR for technology hours and per capita hours. The first two has per capita hours on log level while the last two are on first difference level.

4.7 Conclusions

The evidence from this study shows that hours worked fall or rise after a positive permanent technology shock depending on the empirical treatment of hours. The correlation between technology and hours also indicate a strong positive comovement. Similarly, productivity shows a positive comovement with hours because of positive technology shocks. There is a clear evidence of contraction following the method advocated by Gali (1999). There is no significant contractionary effect present upon positive technology impact, using direct measure of technology or the measure proposed by CEV. The specifications highlights how permanent technology shock causes a hump shaped rise in productivity. This implies that the shocks can account for the strong cyclical positive comovement between hours worked and productivity and as such, it can be concluded that, technology shocks are an important impulse factor.

I show in the tables the corresponding estimates of productivity-labor input correlations conditional (long run restriction imposition) on each type of shock. The BSVAR results also shows the unconditional correlations (short run unrestricted estimation). I presented the results using both Δn_t and $\hat{n}_t$ in the estimated SVAR. The estimates confirm the results from the bivariate model, that technology shocks induce a statistically significant negative correlation between productivity and hours. The figures show the responses of the various variables to a technology shock. The form of responses of productivity, output and employment is very similar to that obtained in the bivariate model. This means that a positive technology shock leads to an increase in productivity but not equal to the proportional change in output. Output's response accumulates more gradually over time. It also means a transitory, though persistent, decline in hours. One noticeable distinction in the figures is that the initial negative effect on hours reversed over time, leading to a positive effect, even though quantitatively small long-term effect.

The concluding key question here is whether technology shocks do generate recognisable business cycles. As indicated by Gali (1999), Chang and Hong (2006) a positive co-movement of GDP and labor input is a key feature of business cycles in industrialized economies. Hence, the answer is affirmative because a positive correlation of output and hours features within the essential predictions of the basic RBC model propelled by technology shocks. It is not explicitly clear if technology shocks are responsible for the pattern of GDP and labor input fluctuations associated with business cycles.

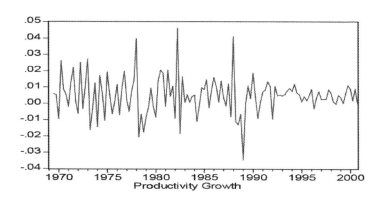

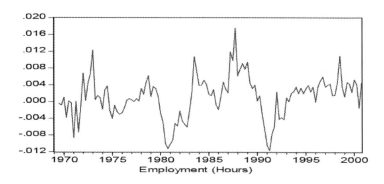

Figure 4.11a: Productivity and Employment

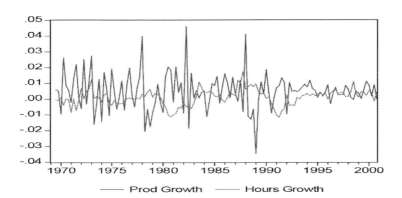

Figure 4.11b: Combined Responses

To understanding the influence on TFP, this empirical research has shed some light through the decomposition of historical time series for GDP and hours or employment into technology and non-technology shocks. I have shown the outcome of this exercise in figures 4.11a and 4.11b. The basis for the above figures came from the bivariate VAR $[\Delta p_t, \Delta n_t]'$. In addition, it shows the estimated growth components of GDP and hours, and the two separately. The fluctuations that the empirical model identifies as having resulted from technology shocks I present among the group of figures in one above. I also obtain similar pattern of results for the de-trended and five-variable models.

Appendix to chapter 4: Model approach

Given the adopted assumptions, the consideration focused on the nominal price rigidities by assuming firm's sets their prices before shocks are realised. Furthermore, the assumption permits for the four key factors in the model namely the household, firm level, monetary and equilibrium to be established.

A4.2.1:   The Households Factor:

The first assumption in the model is that the economy has a population of a large representative family with a continuum of members, where both consumption and hours worked is identical across family members. With this assumption, a representative household would seek to maximise as follows:

$$E_0 \sum_{t=0}^{\infty} \beta^t \left\{ \log C + \lambda_m \log \frac{M_t}{Px_t} - H(N_t, U_t) \right\}$$ Subject to the budget constraint

$$\int_0^1 Px_{it} C_{it} d_i + M_t$$

$$= W_t N_t + V_t U_t + M_{t-1} + \gamma_t + \Pi_t \tag{A4.1}$$

where t = 0, 1,.....n is the time period, C_t is a composite consumption index, Px_{it} is price, M is (nominal) money holdings, H is a function, N is hours and U effort, γ_t is monetary transfer and Π_t denotes profit. W represents the (nominal) price of an hour of work, while V denotes a unit of effort. Thus, the definition of composite consumption as $C_t = \left(\int_0^1 (C_{it})^{\varepsilon-1/\varepsilon} d_i \right)^{\varepsilon/\varepsilon-}$, where, C_{it} is the quantity of goods $i \in [0,1]$ consumed in period t, and $\varepsilon > 1$ is the elasticity of substitution among consumption goods. The price of good i is Px_{it}, expressed as $Px_t = \left(\int_0^1 (Px_{it})^{1-\varepsilon} d_i \right)^{1/1-\varepsilon}$. This is a representation of the aggregate price index, or aggregator. The function H in the equation measures the disutility from work. It also depends on hours (N) and effort (U), hence, the assumption of the form $H(N_t, U_t) = \frac{\lambda_n}{1+\sigma_n} N_t^{1+\sigma_n} + \frac{\lambda_u}{1+\sigma_u} U_t^{1+\sigma_u}$. The expression $\beta \in (0,1)$ is the discount factor while, $\lambda_m, \lambda_n, \lambda_u, \sigma_n, \sigma_u$, are positive constants. This implies the first-order conditions for the household problem can be set as follows: $C_{it} = \left(\frac{Px_{it}}{Px_t}\right)^{-\varepsilon} C_t$ (A4.2)

$$\frac{1}{C_t} = \lambda_m \frac{Px_t}{M_t} + \beta E_t \left[\frac{1}{C_{t+1}} \frac{Px_t}{Px_{t+1}}\right]$$ (A4.3)

$$\frac{W_t}{Px_t} = \lambda_n C_t N_t^{\sigma_n}$$ (A4.4)

$$\frac{V_t}{Px_t} = \lambda_u C_t U_t^{\sigma_u}$$ (A4.5)

Having considered the household level, the next step is to examine the firm level aspect.

A4.2.2: The Firms Level Factor

The second assumption in the model is that each firm have an index $i \in [0,1]$. In other words, the firms are assumed to produce differentiated products with a technology $Y_{it} = T_t L_{it}^{\alpha}$, where L_t is the quantity of effective labor input used and is a function of hours and effort: $L_{it} = N_{it}^{\theta} U_{it}^{1-\theta}$, where $\theta \in (0,1)$ Therefore, the effective labour input is proportional to hours. The term T is an aggregate technology index $T_t = T_{t-1} \exp(\eta_t)$. At the end of period $t-1$ firm i will set the selling price Px_{it} for product i taking as given the aggregate price Px_t (firms in this case are price takers). After the shocks, each firm chooses $_{it}$ and U_{it} that is optimal, given W_t and V_t, including output level Y_{it}, and as such sets the cost minimisation requirement as:

$$\frac{U_{it}}{N_{it}} = \left(\frac{1-\theta}{\theta}\right) \frac{W_t}{V_t} .$$ (A4.6)

Equation (A4.6) demonstrates that, if marginal cost is set below the price level Px_{it}, which has already been determined; each firm will consider it optimal to acknowledge any changes in demand for its product and will accordingly decide an appropriate output level:

$$Y_{it} = \left(\frac{Px_{it}}{Px_t}\right)^{-\varepsilon} C_t .$$
(A4.7)

The implication of this is that, when setting prices, firms will seek to maximise $\max\limits_{P_{it}} E_{t-1}\left\{(1/C_t)(Px_{it}Y_{it} - W_t N_{it} - V_t U_{it})\right\}$ subject to equations (A4.6) & (A4.7) thus, the equivalent first-order condition as:

$$E_{t-1}\left\{(1/C_t)(\alpha\theta Px_{it}Y_{it} - \mu W_t N_{it})\right\} = 0$$
(A4.8)

Here $\mu \equiv \varepsilon / \varepsilon - 1$. It also implies that in the absence of uncertainty, equation (A4.8) will confine to $Px_{it} = \mu(W_t N_{it} / \alpha\theta Y_{it})$. More importantly, it denotes the optimal price condition for a monopolist faced with an iso-elastic demand schedule.

A4.2.3:   The Monetary Policy Factor

The third assumption contained in the model, is the quantity of money M^s in the economy, which we can define as

$$M_t^s = M_{t-1}^s \exp(\xi_t + \gamma\eta_t)$$
(A4.9)

Where $\{\xi_t\}$ is a white noise process orthogonal to $\{\eta_t\}$ at all leads and lags, with $\xi_t \sim N(0, s_m^2)$. Equally, if and only if, $\gamma \neq 0$ the assumption is that the monetary authorities will respond systematically to technology shocks.

A4.2.4:   The Equilibrium Factor

Finally, to have a symmetric equilibrium, all firms in the model will have to set the same price Px_t, while maintaining an identical output, hours and effort levels denoted as Y_t, N_t, U_t. The products (i) market clearing can be represented as $C_t = C_{it} = Y_{it} = Y_t$. This will apply to all demand of a particular variety $i \in [0,1]$ of differentiated products C_{it}, given by $C_{it} = (Px_{it} / Px_t)^{-\eta} C_t$ and for all t. Hence, the equilibrium in the money market will represent $M_t / M_{t-1} = \exp(\xi_t + \gamma \eta_t)$, for all t. The market clearing conditions, equation (A4.3) is set as:

$$C_t = \Phi \frac{M_t}{Px_t} \tag{A4.10}$$

where: $\Phi = \lambda_m^{-1} [1 - \beta \exp\{\tfrac{1}{2}(s_m^2 + \gamma^2 s_z^2)\}]$.

This is assuming $\beta \exp\{\tfrac{1}{2}(s_m^2 + \gamma^2 s_z^2)\} < 1$.

Equally, equations (A4.4), (A4.5) and (A4.6) implies that $U_t = A^{1/\alpha(1-\theta)} N^{(1+\sigma_n)/(1+\sigma_u)}$, where $A \equiv [\lambda_m (1-\theta) / \lambda_u \theta]^{\alpha(1-\theta)/(1+\sigma_u)}$. This allows for the expression of the reduced-form equilibrium relationship between output and employment as:

$$Y_t = AT_t N_t^\phi \tag{A4.11}$$

Here $\phi \equiv \alpha\theta + \alpha(1-\theta)(1+\sigma_n)/(1+\sigma_u)$. By combining equations (A4.4) and (A4.8) with equations (A4.11) and (A4.10) it becomes feasible to obtain the equilibrium levels of price, output, employment and productivity with respect to the exogenous variables. In which case, the lower-case letters denotes the natural logarithm of each variable, while the constants drops out, thereby yielding the equilibrium responses of p_x, y, n, and p to each shock as:

$$\Delta p_{xt} = \xi_{t-1} - (1-\gamma)\eta_{t-1} \tag{A4.12}$$

Where equation (4.12) identifies the equilibrium levels of prices,

$$\Delta y_t = \Delta \xi_t + \gamma \eta_t + (1-\gamma)\eta_{t-1} \tag{A4.13}$$

Equation (4.13) for the equilibrium levels of output,

$$n_t = \frac{1}{\phi}\xi_t - \frac{1-\gamma}{\phi}\eta_t \qquad \text{(A4.14)}$$

Equation (4.14) is the identification for the equilibrium level of employment.

$$\Delta p_t = \left(1 - \frac{1}{\phi}\right)\Delta \xi_t + \left(\frac{1-\gamma}{\phi} + \gamma\right)\eta_t + (1-\gamma)\left(1 - \frac{1}{\phi}\right)\eta_{t-1} \qquad \text{(A4.15)}$$

Finally, equation (A4.15) identifies the equilibrium level for labor productivity, where $p \equiv y - n$ is the log of labor productivity, or, the measured labor productivity. The intuition behind this is that, monetary shocks have a transitory impact on output, employment, productivity and a permanent effect on the price level. Conversely, if there is an unanticipated monetary expansion, $(\xi_t > 0)$ output and employment will rise before returning to their initial level after one period. Under this scenario, the price level would be the only variable with a permanent shock due to the exogenous increase in the money supply.

From equations (A4.13) and (A4.15), a positive technology shock $(\eta_t > 0)$ will have a permanent one to one effect on output and productivity, and a negative effect on the price level if $\gamma < 1$. Equally, if the same condition is satisfied, a positive technology shock will have a negative short run effect on the level of employment. For example, if we assume that there is a constant money supply and a predetermine price, this would signify that real balances remain the same in the period that the technology shock occurs. As a result, each firm will have to achieve its demand by producing an unchanged level of output. In addition, if the technology shocks were positive, to produce the same level of output would need less labour input and a decline in hours. This would mean the sign of the short run response of hours to a technology shock would be in contrast with the RBC model predictions.

Thus, in the following period, firms would react by adjusting their prices downward, since marginal cost is lower. The reaction then leads to a rise in aggregate demand and output, while employment returns to its original level[55]. In terms of the sign for the change in labor productivity, it will depend on whether $\phi \geq, or \leq 1$. Similarly, it will determine if the immediate response of productivity to a technology shock overshoots or not. A possible decline in hours in response to a positive technology shock does not necessarily depend on the assumptions of predetermine prices or the absence of capital accumulation[56]. The computation for the unconditional covariance between the growth rates of output, labor productivity and employment uses equations (A4.12) to (A4.15), to provide the following expressions:

$$\text{cov}\left(\Delta y_t, \Delta n_t\right) = \frac{2s_m^2 + (1-\gamma)(1-2\gamma)s_z^2}{\phi} \tag{A4.16}$$

$$\text{cov}\left(\Delta y_t, \Delta p_t\right) = \frac{2(\phi-1)s_m^2 + (\gamma+\phi-1)s_z^2}{\phi} \tag{A4.17}$$

$$\text{cov}\left(\Delta n_t, \Delta p_t\right) = \frac{2(\phi-1)s_m^2}{\phi^2} - \frac{(1-\gamma)\left[(2-\phi)+2\gamma(\phi-1)\right]s_z^2}{\phi^2} \tag{A4.18}$$

When $\gamma \in \left(0, \frac{1}{2}\right)$ and /or exogenous monetary shocks are sufficient, the model's prediction is that hour's growth will be pro-cyclical and if $\phi > 1$ it is a sufficient condition for measured labor productivity to be pro-cyclical. In terms of the sign of the comovement between hours and productivity growth, it will depend on the size of the ϕ, the policy parameter γ, and the relative significance of shocks. Now, if $\text{cov}\left(\Delta n_t, \Delta p_t / z\right)$ represent the conditional covariance between Δn_t

---

[55] Gali, (1999)

[56] See Rotemberg (1996), in a model of quadratic costs of price adjustment; King and Wolman (1996), in a model with capital accumulation and a price setting structure originally found in Guillermo Calvo (1983). Both of these models reported similar positive responses, however, King and Wolman (1996) also report a negative contemporaneous correlation between multifactor productivity and hours in their calibrated sticky price model with capital accumulation.

and Δp_t conditional on technology as the only source of fluctuation, it will yield the following:

$$\text{cov}\left(\Delta n_t, \Delta p_t / z\right) = -\frac{(1-\gamma)}{\phi^2}\left[(2-\phi)+2\gamma(\phi-1)\right]s_z^2.$$ Note: z denotes shocks from technology, while m denotes shocks from non-technology. Using assumption $\gamma \in [0,1)$ and $\phi \in (1,2)$ it can establish that $\text{cov}\left(\Delta n_t, \Delta x_t / z\right) < 0$, in other words, technology shocks generate a negative comovement between hours and productivity growth. Conversely, the analogous covariance conditional on monetary shocks as the only source of fluctuations represent as $\text{cov}\left(\Delta n_t, \Delta x_t / m\right)$ will yield $\text{cov}\left(\Delta n_t, \Delta x_t / m\right) = \frac{2(\phi-1)}{\phi^2}s_m^2$, where the sign depends on the size of ϕ. If on the other hand $\phi > 1$, monetary shocks is assume to generate a positive comovement between hours and productivity.

The unconditional comovements amid output, hours and productivity are coherent with the RBC model predictions. The model in terms of the conditional comovements between hours and productivity growth has different implications. For example, with technology being the source of fluctuations, the sticky price model predicts a negative correlation between hours and productivity growth, whilst the corresponding comovement conditioned on the non-technology shocks is positive. This contrasts with the RBC model predictions of multiple shocks. This is because technology shocks are assuming as a source of a positive comovement between hours and productivity and non-technology shocks generating a negative comovement.

Notes & Discussions

Notes & Discussions

Chapter 5

Technological Innovations in the UK Private Business Economy: The Effects on Employment and Sectoral Level Estimations

5.0   Introduction

In this chapter, I investigate further the effects of technology as a source of business cycles on employment. The aim is to examine if there is evidence of contractionary effects on UK manufacturing sector (Anyalezu, 2011). The conventional approach has been to look at the path taken by a country's GDP over time, which is not difficult to observe the presence of cycles (R. J Gordon, p.57 (2006)). Under this traditional method, output tends to rise over time. This upward trend is not smooth but punctuated by alternating periods of high and low growth. Thus, economies are characterised by short run fluctuations in economic growth usually referred to as business cycle (Chamberlin & Yueh, 2006, p272). For a more complex model of real business cycle, one can refer to Prescott and Kydland, (1982) seminal paper, or to chapter in Heijdra and Van Der Ploeg (2002) macroeconomics text. Following the expositions in the previous four chapters of this book, there are two main approaches to these cycle namely – Real Business Cycle (RBC) theory and the New Keynesian theories of fluctuations.

This chapter is organised as follows: section 5.1 deals with the technological innovations. Section 5.2 discusses the empirical methodology and outcomes. Section 5.3 analyzes the difference between TFP and labor productivity. Section 5.4 is the conclusion.

5.1   Technological Innovations

In this section, we consider the effect of technological innovations or improvements in the economy, especially, whether it increases or reduces the level of employment that is, contractionary effects. This enables to answer the research question. The empirical analysis focuses on the UK private business economy sectors for evidence.

A number of studies such as Kiley (1998), Gali (1999), Francis and Ramey (2002) and Basu, Fernald and Kimball ((BFK) (2004)), all reported that positive technology shocks might reduce total hours worked in the short run. This is important finding if there is a confirmation of it being the case. The reason is that the fluctuation induced by technological progress may violate a simple fact of RBC model predictions. The RBC model view is that output and employment strongly co-move; see for example Burns and Mitchell (1946). The methodological approach in this chapter therefore adopts the recent method of Chang and Hong (2006) to examine the effects on UK private economy, identified by the permanent components of industry's TFP increases or for evidence of contractionary effects on hours or employment. Evidence from VAR model of the UK private economy sectors for the period 1970 – 2000 shows the effect of technology on employment to vary significantly across sectors on sectoral level. Equally, a good proportion of the sectors indicate a temporary reduction in employment in response to a permanent increase or reduction in TFP. In addition, many sectors exhibits increases in both employment and hours per worker in the short run. The results in this study confirm and/ or are in line with those of Chang and Hong (2006) for the US manufacturing industries (1958 – 1996).

More importantly, this study makes use of actual economy data instead of calibrations as is the normal practices in RBC models, which employs artificial constructed data as a simulation to real economy. For example, in a study by Kiley (1998) he found a strong negative correlation between the permanent component of labor productivity and employment for the US in most two – digit-manufacturing industries. In contrast with Chang et al (2006), the findings are not conflicting because the study identified technology from the permanent components of TFP. In Kiley, technology identification is from those of labor productivity. Thus the debate on whether TFP is perhaps the most appropriate natural measure of technology. The reason is that labor productivity tends to reflect changes in input mix as well as improved efficiency. The objective herein is not about the best approach but the applications in examining the effects on UK private business economy especially in view of the results in chapter 3 of this book where we found no evidence of contractionary effects on aggregate level. However, we discovered some evidence of contraction in chapter 4 of this book while using a different approach. By applying the empirical modelling on sectoral level, a contrasting and significant pictures emerges, which are quite fundamental.

It is possible in this respect to say that, shocks affecting material-labor or capital – labor ratios such as relative input price changes or sectoral reallocation of labor, tend to generate a negative correlation between labor productivity and hours along the downward sloping marginal product of labor, whereas such changes alone do not affect the TFP. The evidence in this study indicates that significant shifts in input mix have taken place in all the sectors. Thus, permanent shocks to input mix are associated with the short run reduction in hours.

Most contractionary effects of technology models with sticky prices, such as in Gali (1999), usually gets acknowledgement. A few other studies in favor of the sticky-price hypothesis include Carlsson (2003) using Swedish manufacturing data, whilst the other is Marchetti and Nucci (2005) on the Italian manufacturing sector. A possible question is, if the variations across sectors on the impact of technology on employment account for by the stickiness of industry output prices. On aggregate as mentioned above, there is no evidence of contractionary effects on impact for the UK private economy sectors. However, when estimated individually sector by sector, a good number of sectors indicate insignificant level of contractionary effects on impact of positive technology shocks. Even when applied to the three distinctly defined hours worked as in the BEID dataset (2003), two sectors; Gas supply and rail transport showed a significant contractionary effect on impact both at 5 percent unconditional level. This is more evident when the sectors are group into nondurable, durable and non-manufacturing sectors. TFP and labor productivity behave distinctly different at the sectoral level. Shocks that affect labor productivity in the long-run do not essential include changes in TFP.

However, imposing a restriction tends to presents a different scenario. More sectors showed contractionary effects at 5 percent significant level. However, when applied using the growth accounting method less sectors showed a contractionary effects when TFP shocks are used.

5.2 The empirical methodology

5.2.1 Data

I derive the industry data from the Bank of England Industry Dataset (BEID) 2003. This includes data on 34 sectors for the period 1969 – 2000. For reasons on data reliability, I utilize data for the period 1970 – 2000. To maintain consistency with the empirical analysis in the previous 4 chapters I restricted the industries to 30 private business economy sectors. The lists of the excluded sectors are in table 5.1 below:

Table 5.1: Excluded Sectors

Sectors SIC92 Industry
1 01, 02, 05 Agriculture
30 75 Public administration and defence
31 80 Education
32 85 Health and Social work

The definition of private business economy is the whole economy less agricultural sector, less public administration and defence, less education, and less health and social work. Further more, the weighted TFP growth is by the industry's revenue. To avoid repetition on procedural approach, please refer to chapters 1 – 4 of this book for further details.

For the three types of hours used, the classifications were as follows: first, hours denoted as (Hrs), which is total hours worked, but not adjusted for quality. In other words, it is a crude sum over males and females, number (weekly number multiple by 52). The second definition of the data, the total hours worked denoted as LABQA. I used labor input which is the total hours worked, adjusted (by the Bank of England) for quality using the Pablo and Jerry's measure where the Fisher index, = 1 in 1995. The third is labor input (LAB), the total hours worked but not adjusted for quality.

5.3   Permanent Technology Shocks Identification

The identification of permanent technology shock is through the structural vector autoregression (SVAR) model of industry TFP and hours worked. The fluctuations in industry TFP and hours worked are driven by two underlying disturbances – technology and nontechnology shocks. These are orthogonal to each other. The assumption is that only permanent shock can have a permanent effect on the level of industry productivity. The other assumption is that both technology and nontechnology shocks can have a permanent effect on industry hours. For simplicity purpose, the assumption is that nontechnology shocks consist of aggregate such as monetary shocks and/or sectoral reallocation shocks. It is therefore not necessary to make any further interpretation.

5.4   The Methodology

The methodological technique is the same as in Gali (1999), BFK (2004), which I employ in chapter 4. I therefore in this chapter, follow Chang and Hong (2006) approach that uses Blanchard and Quah decomposition (1989)[57] and employ TFP and BFK growth accounting method instead of productivity output. Hence, it is possible to show the vector Δp_t, as $\left[\Delta t_t, \Delta n_t \right]$, where Δt_t and Δn_t denotes TFP growth and labor hour's growth and BFK-hours respectively, both the unconditional and conditional estimates. Equally, the term ε_t is the vector of the two shocks, which we can express as: $\left[\varepsilon_t^z, \varepsilon_t^l \right]'$ where ε_t^z and ε_t^l are technology and nontechnology shocks respectively.

For the data used, both the TFP and hours, and the BFK-hours are integrated of order one. In addition, Δp_t is a distributed lag of both types of shocks and a simplified format of it is as follow:

$$\Delta p_t = C(L)\varepsilon_t = \sum_{j=0}^{\infty} C_j \varepsilon_{t-j} \tag{1}$$

Where $E[\varepsilon_t \varepsilon_t'] = 1$, and $E[\varepsilon_t \varepsilon_s'] = 0, t \neq s$. Note the suppression of constant terms in the shocks is for expositional convenience purposes

---

[57] Blanchard, O. and Quah, D. (1989), "The dynamic effects of aggregate supply and demand disturbances", American Economic Review 79, 655 – 673

only. The identifying restriction is: $C^{12}(1) = \sum_{j=0}^{\infty} C_j^{12} = 0$. Thus, we have the MA representation as:

$$\Delta p_t = A(L)e_t$$

$$= \sum_{j=0}^{\infty} A_j e_{t-j} \tag{2}$$

Thus, $A_0 = 1$

$$E\left[e_t e_t'\right] = \Omega_,$$

$$E\left[e_t e_s'\right] = 0, t \neq s$$

$$\Omega = C_0 C_0',$$

$$e_t = C_0 \varepsilon_t$$

$$C_j = A_j C_0 .$$

The MA representation $A(L)$ came from the VAR of:

$$\Delta p_t = B(L)\Delta p_{t-1} + e_t$$

$$= \sum_{j=1}^{P} B_j \Delta p_{t-j} + e_t \tag{3}$$

The estimated equation is the VAR (3) for the aggregates. The other possibility is to estimate pooled specifications on disaggregated data, and restricting coefficients identical across sectors. The expression can be as follows:

$$\Delta p_t^i = B(L)\Delta p_{t-1}^i + e_t \quad i = 1 \ldots \ldots \ldots N . \tag{4}$$

Where, N is the number of sub-industries or subsectors. The assumption is that $B(L)$ and Ω is the same across the subsectors but allowing for different average growth rates in TFP and hours, or the BFK- hours. The aggregate private economy is the durables, nondurable, non-manufacturing sectors. The aggregates of the three subsectors are also separately stated. The empirical modelling is base on aggregate data. All the VARs have a lag of two and in first difference level – growth years[58]. I covered extensively the issues surrounding the treatment of hours as stationary in levels or in first difference in chapter 4, hence, no need repeating them in this chapter. I therefore apply the first difference in the estimations in this chapter.

The reason for the adopted treatment is that, whichever one applies, there is not much difference as far as the UK data is concerned. In addition, Christiano et al (2003) and my analysis in the previous chapter discussed this at length. For stationarity, again it is adequately analyse in previous chapters. For further insight, one can refer to Shapiro and Watson (1988). The main reason for discussing stationarity is the balanced growth path at the aggregate level. For the case of economy or sector level, a permanent change in productivity may imply a long run change in hours worked through sectoral reallocation of labour. Hours in any case tends to be nonstationary in some industries. In that respect, a possible assumption is to reject the null hypothesis of unit root at 10 percent significance level. In which case, it is justifiable to treat hours at first difference in this empirical analysis of sectoral VARs.

5.5   The Results

Lets' begin by examining the impulse responses from the SVAR on TFP and hours worked. The figure 1 below shows the impulse responses of TFP and hours for the aggregate economy sectors (A). This is a response

---

[58] The Akaike Information Criterion (AIC) the optimal lag length is 2 and the Schwartz Information Criterion (SIC) also choose 2 lag length.

to Cholesky one S.D innovations ± 2S.E. In other words, a response to a one standard deviation technology shock, increases the private economy sectors TFP, hours worked increases 0.67 percent on impact but decline to 0.15 percent in year 1. Hours worked continue to rise in year two and three reaching a new steady state of 0.003 percent higher than before. For the bivariate estimate at aggregate private economy level, hours increased by 1.14 percent on technology shock and by 1.02 percent in response to nontechnology shock, while TFP increases by 0.89 and 0.72 percent respectively. This implies that TFP has procyclical factor utilization and then returns to the previous level over time. It is also similar pattern of responses on the pooled disaggregate data, that is, durable and nondurable manufacturing sectors ((B) and (C)) of figure 1.

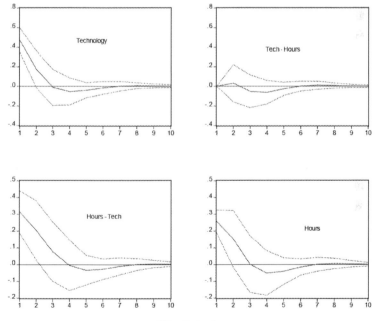

Fig.5.1: A

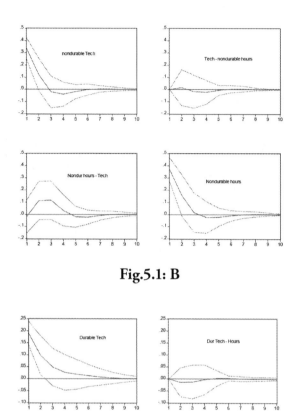

Fig.5.1: B

Fig.5.1: C

Figure 5.1: (A) Aggregate private economy impulse responses of TFP and Hours; (B) Aggregate nondurable manufacturing sector TFP and Hours responses, (C) Aggregate durable manufacturing sector responses of TFP and Hours

In table 5.2, I display the results of the estimation of hours on current and lagged TFP growth. Here I employ the technique advocated by BFK (2004) in the regression estimation. Table 5.3.1 – 5.3.3 is the unconditional and decomposed long run conditional correlation estimates of TFP growth and hours worked growth, while table 5.4.1 – 5.4.3 is the BFK TFP and hours for unconditional and conditional correlation estimates. On aggregate manufacturing level, the general growth rates of TFP and hours worked correlates strongly and positively. To compute the long run, that is, conditional correlation on technology based on SVAR estimates, I adopt the Gali (1999) approach:

$$Corr(\Delta t_t, \Delta n_t / \varepsilon^i) = \frac{\sum_{j=0}^{\infty} C_j^{1i} C_j^{2i}}{\sqrt{\mathrm{var}(\Delta t_t / \varepsilon^i) \bullet \mathrm{var}(\Delta n_t / \varepsilon^i)}}, \text{ for } i = t, n$$

Where $\mathrm{var}(\Delta t_t / \varepsilon^i) = \sum_{j=0}^{\infty} (C_j^{1i})^2$ and $\mathrm{var}(\Delta n_t / \varepsilon^i) = \sum_{j=0}^{\infty} (C_j^{2i})^2$.

The results are in the tables below.

Level Estimations: U.K Private Economy Sectors

Table 5.2:   Regressions on current and lagged (TFP) technology shocks Δt

Dep Var Sectors Δn	Δt	$\Delta t(-1)$	$\Delta t(-2)$	$\Delta t(-3)$	$\Delta t(-4)$	R^2	DW-Stat
Agg Manuf Δn	**0.67** (5.24)	**-0.15** (-0.76)	**0.13** (0.68)	**0.003** (0.02)	**-0.05** (-0.36)	**0.73**	**2.11**
2	0.059 (0.22)	0.213 (0.93)	0.028 (0.12)	0.257 (1.44)	0.67 (0.36)	0.43	1.86
3	-0.15 (-0.72)	-0.19 (-0.87)	0.12 (0.56)	0.02 (0.09)	0.04 (0.21)	0.43	1.42
4	-0.25 (-0.93)	0.29 (1.12)	-0.23 (-0.73)	0.31 (1.08)	-0.37 (-1.33)	0.14	2.33
5	0.09 (0.47)	0.43 (2.28)	0.06 (0.33)	-0.16 (-0.81)	0.10 (0.53)	0.28	1.63

6	0.33 (1.38)	0.30 (1.18)	-0.07 (-0.27)	-0.17 (-0.69)	-0.08 (-0.37)	0.54	2.02
7	0.10 (0.61)	0.49 (2.92)	-0.55 (-2.76)	-0.08 (-0.48)	0.26 (1.81)	0.65	1.89
8	0.50 (1.77)	-0.18 (-0.63)	0.21 (0.86)	0.14 (0.46)	0.19 (0.72)	0.51	2.07
9	0.14 (0.62)	0.19 (0.78)	0.01 (0.04)	-0.71 (-3.10)	0.29 (1.38)	0.66	1.66
10	0.11 (0.31)	0.16 (0.39)	-0.06 (-0.16)	-0.12 (-0.30)	0.10 (0.24)	0.28	1.88
11	-0.70 (-1.82)	0.28 (0.65)	0.10 (0.23)	-0.22 (-0.58)	0.02 (0.08)	0.17	1.66
12	0.37 (1.37)	0.86 (2.87)	-0.22 (-0.59)	-0.23 (-0.63)	-0.07 (-0.22)	0.64	1.97
13	0.22 (1.56)	0.49 (3.54)	-0.04 (-0.28)	-0.01 (-0.06)	0.13 (-1.05)	0.54	1.96
14	0.54 (2.94)	0.19 (0.83)	-0.35 (-1.51)	-0.04 (-0.17)	0.13 (0.72)	0.66	1.92
15	0.15 (0.68)	0.27 (1.23)	0.18 (0.84)	0.24 (1.14)	-0.16 (-0.78)	0.14	2.33
16	0.01 (0.03)	-0.86 (-1.60)	-0.03 (-0.05)	0.14 (0.28)	-0.05 (-0.12)	0.22	1.89
17	-1.91 (-4.89)	1.16 (2.20)	0.02 (0.03)	0.31 (0.65)	1.25 (2.70)	0.72	2.05
18	0.67 (2.28)	0.40 (1.25)	0.09 (0.26)	-0.25 (-0.79)	-0.30 (-1.03)	0.54	1.74
19	0.03 (0.18)	0.22 (1.26)	-0.04 (-0.21)	-0.17 (-0.96)	-0.03 (-0.14)	0.28	1.57
20	-0.20 (-1.52)	0.53 (3.92)	-0.13 (-0.79)	0.09 (0.71)	-0.11 (-1.09)	0.58	1.86
21	-0.272 (-1.37)	0.285 (1.15)	-0.155 (-0.63)	0.234 (0.97)	-0.393 (-2.11)	0.37	1.87
22	-1.412 (-4.64)	-0.679 (-2.13)	0.236 (0.78)	0.198 (0.65)	-0.513 (-1.75)	0.66	1.86
23	-0.689 (-2.41)	0.57 (1.93)	0.31 (1.14)	0.456 (1.56)	-0.095 (-0.30)	0.49	1.77
24	-0.35 (-1.13)	0.656 (1.95)	-0.332 (-0.98)	-0.124 (-0.36)	-0.342 (-1.04)	0.39	1.87
25	-0.151 (-0.62)	0.62 (2.37)	-0.134 (-0.48)	0.156 (0.58)	-0.099 (-0.39)	0.50	1.62
26	-0.26 (-1.19)	0.347 (1.74)	0.04 (0.19)	-0.099 (-0.46)	0.197 (1.05)	0.37	1.75

24	-0.35	0.656	-0.332	-0.124	-0.342	0.39	1.87
	(-1.13)	(1.95)	(-0.98)	(-0.36)	(-1.04)		
25	-0.151	0.62	-0.134	0.156	-0.099	0.50	1.62
	(-0.62)	(2.37)	(-0.48)	(0.58)	(-0.39)		
26	-0.26	0.347	0.04	-0.099	0.197	0.37	1.75
	(-1.19)	(1.74)	(0.19)	(-0.46)	(1.05)		
27	-0.294	0.199	0.356	0.314	0.330	0.53	2.03
	(-1.67)	(1.04)	(1.92)	(1.85)	(1.97)		
28	-0.526	0.284	0.026	-0.042	0.341	0.55	1.57
	(-2.89)	(1.24)	(0.11)	(-0.19)	(1.69)		
29	-0.239	0.103	-0.011	-0.156	0.113	0.37	1.81
	(-1.09)	(0.44)	(-0.05)	(-0.69)	(0.55)		
33	-0.259	0.255	0.259	0.525	0.079	0.24	1.38
	(-0.63)	(0.56)	(0.56)	(1.15)	(0.18)		
34	-0.729	0.936	-0.274	0.352	-0.197	0.56	1.97
	(-3.12)	(3.06)	(-0.82)	(1.49)	(-0.89)		
Agg. Non durable	**-0.013**	**0.52**	**0.08**	**-0.15**	**0.18**	**0.37**	**1.83**
	(-0.05)	**(1.94)**	**(0.30)**	**(-0.53)**	**(0.67)**		
Agg. Durable	**0.52**	**0.11**	**-0.12**	**-0.13**	**0.11**	**0.65**	**1.91**
	(2.71)	**(0.46)**	**(-0.51)**	**(-0.53)**	**(0.58)**		

Note: All the dependent variables are in growth rate. Each sector represents a separate OLS regression. Some variables or sector hours growth (Δn) were corrected for endogeneity. The parentheses in brackets are t-statistic

On the disaggregate level, aggregate nondurable manufacturing sectors shows a contraction on impact of -0.013 percent and a t-statistic of -0.05 percent but returns to strong positive increase of 0.52 percent (t-statistic of (1.94)) in year one and another rise in second year before declining again in the third year. The aggregate durable manufacturing on the other hand has an increase in hours worked of 0.52 percent and a t-statistic of 2.71 percent on impact and in year one of 0.11 percent and t-statistic of 0.46 percent. In terms of the individual sectors, almost all the nondurable manufacturing sectors using BFK-hours has a contractionary effect on impact (table 5.4.1) after a positive technology shocks. Table 5.2.1 below shows the total number of industries exhibiting contractionary effect in types of industries: durable manufacturing, nondurable manufacturing and non-manufacturing sector. The concentration of industries showing contractionary effect is on the non-manufacturing sector while there was none in the durable manufacturing sector.

Table 5.2.1: Industries showing Contractionary Effect by Sectors

Total Number of sectors	16	SIC No.	Sectors
Durable Manufacturing	Nil	n/a	nil
Non-Durable	3	3	Coal & other mining
		4	Manufactured fuel
		11	Food, drink & tobacco
Non Manufacturing	13	17	Water supply
		20	Retailing
		21	Hotels & catering
		22	Rail transport
		23	Road transport
		24	Water transport
		25	Air transport
		26	Other transport services
		27	Communications
		28	Finance
		29	Business services
		33	Waste treatment
		34	Miscellaneous services

In regards to the results obtained on the sectoral estimations, intuitively, one would expect contractionary effects to be more significant in capital-intensive industries, but the results suggest otherwise. Thus, it is possible to look again at the relation to sticky prices and the RBC explanations. A negative response is inconsistent with the prediction of the baseline flexible-price model, as I explained in chapter 1. According to Jermann (1998), with adjustment costs to investment, a RBC model with flexible prices can exhibit a negative response of hours to technology. Gali (1999), on the other hand, proposed a sticky-price model as a mechanism capable of generating a negative impact of technology on employment.

Therefore, intuitively, when price is fixed, the demand for goods remains unchanged, and firms need less input including labour, to produce the same amount of output as a result of improved efficiency.

BFK (2004) in reaching to the conclusion that in the short run, technology improvements significantly reduce input use and non-residential investment argued that the results are inconsistent with standard parameterisations of RBC models, which imply that technology improvements raise input use at all horizons. Hence, they maintained the view given the results of a consistency with the predictions of dynamic general equilibrium models with sticky price output prices driven by both technology and monetary shocks.

In addition, Dotsey (2002) and Gali et al (2003) show that technology's effect on employment also depends on monetary policy. This means that, employment can increase even under the sticky-price model if the monetary authority strongly accommodates technology shocks. In this case, the sticky-price explanation appears to work best with respect to the results reported in this thesis and as such is the preferable one.

Table 5.3.1 TFP/ Hours

SIC Industry	$cor(\Delta t, \Delta n)$	$cor(\Delta t, \Delta n / \varepsilon^z)$	$cor(\Delta t, \Delta n / \varepsilon^m)$
Aggregate manufacturing	0.59	-0.10	0.39
	(0.29)	(-0.28)	(1.65)*
Nondurables	0.14	-0.1	0.67
	(0.63)	(-0.01)	(1.22)
2 Oil & Gas 11, 12	0.32	0.90	-0.62
	(1.80)*	(2.36)**	(-1.40)
3 Coal & other mining 10, 13,14	-0.08	-1.64	0.39
	(-0.43)	(-0.24)	(0.93)

4 Manufactured fuel 23	-0.15	-0.48	-0.76
	(-0.73)	(-0.65)	(-1.02)
5 Chemicals & pharmaceutical 24	0.18	0.20	0.73
	(0.81)	(0.43)	(1.04)
11 Food, drink & tobacco 15, 16	0.04	0.03	0.64
	(0.19)	(0.05)	(1.15)
12 Textiles, clothing & leather 17, 18, 19	0.29	0.33	-0.74
	(1.19)	(0.77)	(-1.08)
13 Paper, printing & publishing 21, 22	-0.11	-0.22	0.36
	(-0.68)	(-0.87)	(1.64)
Durables	0.49	0.65	0.77
	(2.24)**	(1.65)*	(1.39)
6 non-metallic mineral products 26	0.13	0.16	0.63
	(0.57)	(0.26)	(1.01)
7 Basic metals & metal goods 27, 28	0.27	0.32	0.74
	(1.196)	(0.56)	(1.12)
8 Mechanical engineering 29	-0.05	-0.25	0.63
	(-0.24)	(-0.40)	(1.38)
9 Electrical engineering & electronics 30, 31, 32, 33	-0.13	-0.04	-0.50
	(-0.61)	(-0.095)	(-1.77)*
10 Vehicles 34, 35	0.27	0.38	0.76
	(1.09)	(0.55)	(1.07)
14 Other manufacturing 20, 25, 36,37	0.18	0.198	0.69
	(0.91)	(0.41)	(1.13)
19 Wholesale, vehicle sales & repairs 50, 51	0.11	0.15	0.68
	(0.51)	(0.21)	(0.84)
Non-manufacturing	0.05	-0.27	0.53
	(0.27)	(-0.56)	(1.16)
15 Electrical supply 40.1	-0.25	-0.44	-0.67
	(-1.31)	(-0.67)	(-1.30)
16 Gas Supply 40.2, 40.3	0.57	-0.60	0.84
	(-2.57)**	(-1.67)*	(1.05)
17 Water supply 41	0.39	0.41	-0.69
	(1.45)	(0.82)	(-1.29)
18 Construction 45	0.24	0.25	0.70
	(1.21)	(0.71)	(1.22)
20 Retailing 52	0.06	0.06	0.36
	(0.28)	(0.12)	(0.76)
21 Hotels & catering 55	0.24	0.40	-0.795
	(0.92)	(0.58)	(-1.05)

22 Rail transport 60.1	-0.49	-0.57	0.76
	(-2.09)**	(-1.01)	(1.03)
23 Road transport 60.2, 60.3	-0.06	-0.03	- 0.58
	(0.26)	(-0.06)	(-1.15)
24 Water transport 61	0.06	0.21	-0.75
	(0.26)	(0.34)	(-1.31)
25 Air transport 62	0.24	0.25	0.61
	(1.01)	(0.49)	(1.10)
26 Other transport services 63	0.14	0.32	-0.79
	(0.58)	(0.87)	(-2.66)**
27 Communications 64	0.05	0.001	0.54
	(0.26)	(0.003)	(1.89)*
28 Finance 65, 66	-0.00	-0.16	0.52
	(-0.00)	(-0.33)	(1.56)
29 Business services	-0.15	-0.698	0.55
67, 70, 71, 72, 73, 74	(-0.63)	(-1.22)	(1.42)
33 Waste treatment 90	-0.07	-0.16	-0.69
	(-0.34)	(-0.22)	(-1.01)
34 Miscellaneous services 91-99	0.39	0.45	-0.73
	(1.68)*	(1.17)	(-1.05)

The t statistics are in parentheses bracket. The level of significance is denoted by the asterisks (*) & (**) at 10% and 5% respectively. The U.K private economy

Table 5.3.2 TFP/ LAB

SIC Industry	$cor(\Delta t, \Delta n)$	$cor(\Delta t, \Delta n / \varepsilon^z)$	$cor(\Delta t, \Delta n / \varepsilon^m)$
Aggregate manufacturing	0.297	0.29	0.58
	(1.39)	(0.72)	(0.58)
Nondurables	0.14	-0.01	0.67
	(0.66)	(-0.01)	(1.23)
2 Oil & Gas 11, 12	0.32	0.90	-0.62
	(1.72)*	(2.31)**	(-1.39)
3 Coal & other mining 10, 13,14	-0.08	-0.16	0.39
	(-0.39)	(-0.24)	(0.92)

4 Manufactured fuel 23	-0.15	-0.48	-0.76
	(-0.80)	(-0.65)	(-1.01)
5 Chemicals & pharmaceutical 24	0.18	0.20\	0.73
	(0.84)	(0.41)	(1.07)
11 Food, drink & tobacco 15, 16	0.04	0.03	0.64
	(0.19)	(0.04)	(1.12)
12 Textiles, clothing & leather 17, 18, 19	0.29	0.33	-0.74
	(1.25)	(0.76)	(-1.09)
13 Paper, printing & publishing 21, 22	-0.11	-0.22	0.36
	(-0.65)	(-0.88)	(1.76)*
Durables	0.49	0.65	0.77
	(2.21)**	(1.62)	(1.43)
6 non-metallic mineral products 26	0.13	0.16	0.63
	(0.56)	(0.26)	(1.01)
7 Basic metals & metal goods 27, 28	0.27	0.32	0.74
	(1.23)	(0.57)	(1.13)
8 Mechanical engineering 29	-0.05	-0.25	0.63
	(-0.23)	(-0.41)	(1.44)
9 Electrical engineering & electronics 30, 31, 32, 33	-0.13	-0.04	-0.50
	(-0.62)	(-0.097)	(-1.85)*
10 Vehicles 34, 35	0.27	0.38	0.76
	(1.05)	(0.55)	(1.08)
14 Other manufacturing 20, 25, 36,37	0.18	0.198	0.69
	(0.90)	(0.41)	(1.14)
19 Wholesale, vehicle sales & repairs 50, 51	0.11	0.15	0.68
	(0.52)	(0.21)	(0.85)
Non-manufacturing	0.05	-0.27	0.53
	(0.26)	(-0.57)	(1.15)
15 Electrical supply 40.1	-0.25	-0.44	-0.66
	(-1.25)	(-0.65)	(-1.23)
16 Gas Supply 40.2, 40.3	-0.57	-0.60	0.84
	(-2.47)**	(-1.64)	(1.05)
17 Water supply 41	0.39	0.41	-0.69
	(1.38)	(0.78)	(-1.31)
18 Construction 45	0.24	0.25	0.70
	(1.20)	(0.71)	(1.17)
20 Retailing 52	0.06	0.06	0.36
	(0.28)	(0.13)	(0.78)
21 Hotels & catering 55	0.24	0.40	-0.795
	(0.88)	(0.58)	(-1.04)

22 Rail transport 60.1	-0.49	0.57	0.76
	(-2.097)**	(-1.01)	(1.03)
23 Road transport 60.2, 60.3	-0.06	-0.03	-0.58
	(-0.24)	(-0.06)	(-1.15)
24 Water transport 61	0.06	0.21	-0.75
	(0.29)	(0.35)	(-1.30)
25 Air transport 62	0.24	0.25	0.61
	(1.01)	(0.497)	(1.13)
26 Other transport services 63	0.14	0.32	-0.79
	(0.57)	(0.84)	(-2.64)**
27 Communications 64	0.05	0.00	0.54
	(0.26)	(0.00)	(1.67)*
28 Finance 65, 66	-0.00	-0.16	0.52
	(-0.00)	(-0.33)	(1.48)
29 Business services	-0.15	-0.698	0.55
67, 70, 71, 72, 73, 74	(-0.64)	(-1.22)	(1.33)
33 Waste treatment 90	-0.07	-0.16	-0.69
	(-0.35)	(0.21)	(-1.01)
34 Miscellaneous services 91-99	0.39	0.45	-0.73
	(1.73)*	(1.11)	(-1.04)

The level of significance is denoted by the asterisks (*) & (**) at 10% and 5% respectively. The U.K private economy

Table 5.3.3 TFP/ LABQA

SIC Industry	$cor(\Delta t, \Delta n)$	$cor(\Delta t, \Delta n / \varepsilon^z)$	$cor(\Delta t, \Delta n / \varepsilon^m)$
Aggregate manufacturing	0.29	0.32	0.65
	(1.37)	(0.71)	(1.39)
Nondurables	0.11	-0.23	0.71
	(0.54)	(-0.35)	(1.21)
2 Oil & Gas 11, 12	0.33	0.92	-0.62
	(1.74)*	(2.33)**	(-1.34)
3 Coal & other mining 10, 13,14	-0.08	-0.18	0.41
	(-0.42)	(-0.26)	(0.96)
4 Manufactured fuel 23	-0.18	-0.70	-0.76
	(-0.91)	(-0.95)	(-1.03)

5 Chemicals & pharmaceutical	0.15	0.19	-0.77
24	(0.70)	(0.36)	(-1.03)
11 Food, drink & tobacco 15, 16	-0.06	-0.17	0.68
	(-0.33)	(-0.27)	(1.20)
12 Textiles, clothing & leather	0.29	0.33	-0.77
17, 18, 19	(1.24)	(0.74)	(-1.10)
13 Paper, printing & publishing	-0.11	-0.22	0.44
21, 22	(-0.59)	(-0.73)	(2.01)**
Durables	0.49	0.73	0.81
	(2.10)**	(1.76)*	(1.25)
6 non-metallic mineral products	0.11	0.15	-0.64
26	(0.46)	(0.23)	(-0.99)
7 Basic metals & metal goods	0.58	0.48	0.68
27, 28	(2.57)**	(-0.88)	(0.92)
8 Mechanical engineering 29	-0.04	-0.20	0.66
	(-0.17)	(-0.34)	(1.45)
9 Electrical engineering &	-0.16	-0.13	-0.53
electronics 30, 31, 32, 33	(0.71)	(-0.31)	(-1.94)*
10 Vehicles 34, 35	0.29	0.40	0.79
	(1.14)	(0.59)	(1.08)
14 Other manufacturing	0.16	0.19	0.71
20, 25, 36,37	(0.72)	(0.36)	(1.03)
19 Wholesale, vehicle sales &	0.22	0.28	-0.05
repairs 50, 51	(1.02)	(0.41)	(-0.06)
Non-manufacturing	0.03	-0.33	0.57
	(0.13)	(-0.68)	(1.26)
15 Electrical supply 40.1	-0.24	-0.57	-0.67
	(-1.20)	(-0.81)	(-1.11)
16 Gas Supply 40.2, 40.3	-0.57	-0.60	0.85
	(-2.70)**	(1.74)*	(1.04)
17 Water supply 41	0.44	0.47	-0.72
	(1.59)	(0.95)	(-1.27)
18 Construction 45	0.25	0.26	0.71
	(1.15)	(0.70)	(1.19)
20 Retailing 52	0.16	0.21	-0.71
	(0.64)	(0.63)	(-2.54)**
21 Hotels & catering 55	0.13	0.34	-0.82
	(0.49)	(0.47)	(-1.06)
22 Rail transport 60.1	-0.49	-0.57	0.77
	(-2.08)**	(-1.01)	(1.03)

23 Road transport 60.2, 60.3	-0.05	-0.02	-0.58
	(-0.21)	(-0.05)	(-1.17)
24 Water transport 61	0.08	0.22	-0.76
	(0.34)	(0.35)	(-1.29)
25 Air transport 62	0.23	0.24	0.60
	(0.97)	(0.48)	(1.13)
26 Other transport services 63	0.16	0.36	-0.81
	(0.64)	(1.07)	(-3.17)**
27 Communications 64	0.14	0.14	0.63
	(0.63)	(0.26)	(1.20)
28 Finance 65, 66	-0.00	-0.16	0.64
	(-0.00)	(-0.30)	(1.68)*
29 Business services	-0.20	-0.99	0.58
67, 70, 71, 72, 73, 74	(-0.87)	(-1.69)*	(1.39)
33 Waste treatment 90	-0.04	-0.05	-0.67
	(-0.17)	(-0.07)	(-1.01)
34 Miscellaneous services 91-99	0.46	0.53	-0.82
	(2.15)**	(1.44)	(-1.24)

The level of significance is denoted by the asterisks (*) & (**) at 10% and 5% respectively. The U.K private economy

Table 5.4.1 BFK Hours

SIC Industry	$cor(\Delta t, \Delta n)$	$cor(\Delta t, \Delta n / \varepsilon^z)$	$cor(\Delta t, \Delta n / \varepsilon^m)$
Aggregate manufacturing	0.98	0.95	0.99
	(5.08)**	(5.48)**	(3.47)**
Nondurables	-0.18	-0.99	0.34
	(-0.98)	(-4.92)**	(1.62)
2 Oil & Gas 11, 12	0.15	0.99	-0.61
	(0.79)	(1.41)	(-1.09)
3 Coal & other mining 10, 13,14	-0.14	-0.24	0.43
	(-0.70)	(-0.35)	(0.94)
4 Manufactured fuel 23	-0.24	-0.60	0.78
	(-1.17)	(-0.87)	(1.06)
5 Chemicals & pharmaceutical 24	0.21	0.98	-0.57
	(0.95)	(4.77)**	(-2.32)**

11 Food, drink & tobacco 15, 16	-0.28	-0.99	0.72
	(-1.29)	(-4.06)**	(3.59)**
12 Textiles, clothing & leather 17, 18, 19	0.91	0.67	0.99
	(4.37)**	(1.05)	(2.40)**
13 Paper, printing & publishing 21, 22	-0.44	-0.18	-0.64
	(-2.11)**	(-0.88)	(-2.47)**
Durables	0.06	-0.10	0.40
	(0.30)	(-0.30)	(1.76)*
6 non-metallic mineral products 26	-0.34	-0.85	0.47
	(-1.68)*	(-4.77)**	(1.57)
7 Basic metals & metal goods 27, 28	0.19	0.95	-0.41
	(0.93)	(5.06)**	(-1.34)
8 Mechanical engineering 29	-0.75	-0.64	-0.81
	(-3.83)**	(-3.81)**	(-2.88)**
9 Electrical engineering & electronics 30, 31, 32, 33	-0.13	-0.57	-0.42
	(-0.68)	(-0.83)	(-0.98)
10 Vehicles 34, 35	0.00	0.80	-0.29
	(0.00)	(4.45)**	(-1.34)
14 Other manufacturing 20, 25, 36,37	-0.17	-0.71	0.45
	(-0.87)	(-2.28)**	(2.08)**
19 Wholesale, vehicle sales & repairs 50, 51	-0.02	-0.46	- 0.68
	(-0.87)	(1.25)	(-0.97)
Non-manufacturing	0.84	0.60	0.99
	(3.96)**	(2.83)**	(4.17)**
15 Electrical supply 40.1	0.22	0.81	-0.54
	(1.15)	(3.15)**	(-2.98)
16 Gas Supply 40.2, 40.3	-0.17	-0.38	0.61
	(-0.85)	(-0.55)	(1.13)
17 Water supply 41	-0.26	-0.62	0.34
	(-1.28)	(-2.67)**	(1.47)
18 Construction 45	-0.05	0.98	-0.46
	(-0.29)	(5.85)**	(-1.89)
20 Retailing 52	-0.16	0.94	-0.68
	(-0.87)	(1.25)	(-0.97)
21 Hotels & catering 55	-0.12	-0.14	-0.50
	(-0.59)	(0.29)	(-1.74)*
22 Rail transport 60.1	-0.79	-0.92	-0.77
	(-4.00)**	(-1.40)	(-1.73)*
23 Road transport 60.2, 60.3	-0.31	-0.99	0.50
	(-1.51)	(-4.66)**	(2.10)**

24 Water transport 61	0.56	0.99	-0.23
	(2.55)**	(4.64)**	(-0.69)
25 Air transport 62	-0.08	-0.99	0.36
	(-0.38)	(-4.86)**	(1.60)
26 Other transport services 63	-0.26	-0.99	0.59
	(-1.25)	(-4.21)**	(2.93)**
27 Communications 64	-0.06	0.97	-0.62
	(-0.27)	(4.69)**	(-2.45)**
28 Finance 65, 66	0.07	0.95	-0.52
	(0.33)	(5.09)**	(-1.83)*
29 Business services	-0.35	-0.70	-0.31
67, 70, 71, 72, 73, 74	(-1.68)*	(-3.60)**	(-0.97)
33 Waste treatment 90	-0.00	-0.93	0.62
	(-0.01)	(-1.59)	(1.52)
34 Miscellaneous services 91-99	0.25	-0.99	0.73
	(1.22)	(-4.95)**	(3.15)**

The level of significance is denoted by the asterisks (*) & (**) at 10% and 5% respectively. The U.K private economy

Table 5.4.2 BFK LAB

SIC Industry	$cor(\Delta t, \Delta n)$	$cor(\Delta t, \Delta n / \varepsilon^z)$	$cor(\Delta t, \Delta n / \varepsilon^m)$
Aggregate manufacturing	0.98	0.95	0.99
	(4.76)**	(5.21)**	(3.37)**
Nondurables	-0.18	-0.99	0.34
	(-0.96)	(-5.33)**	(1.49)
2 Oil & Gas 11, 12	0.15	0.99	-0.61
	(0.82)	(1.36)	(-1.09)
3 Coal & other mining 10, 13,14	-0.14	-0.24	0.43
	(0.68)	(0.35)	(0.94)
4 Manufactured fuel 23	-0.24	-0.60	0.78
	(-1.28)	(-0.88)	(1.06)
5 Chemicals & pharmaceutical 24	0.21	0.98	-0.57
	(0.96)	(4.94)**	(-2.08)**
11 Food, drink & tobacco 15, 16	-0.28	-0.99	0.72
	(-1.37)	(-4.79)**	(3.52)**
12 Textiles, clothing & leather	0.91	0.67	0.99

17, 18, 19	(4.21)**	(1.05)	(2.38)**
13 Paper, printing & publishing	-0.44	-0.18	-0.64
21, 22	(-2.02)**	(-0.84)	(-2.38)**
Durables	0.06	-0.10	0.40
	(0.29)	(-0.31)	(1.74)*
6 non-metallic mineral products	-0.34	-0.85	0.47
26	(-1.69)*	(-4.84)**	(1.63)
7 Basic metals & metal goods	0.19	0.94	-0.41
27, 28	(1.02)	(5.73)**	(-1.34)
8 Mechanical engineering 29	-0.75	-0.64	-0.81
	(-3.52)**	(-3.29)**	(-2.71)**
9 Electrical engineering & electronics	-0.13	-0.57	-0.42
30, 31, 32, 33	(-0.72)	(-0.82)	(-1.01)
10 Vehicles 34, 35	0.00	0.81	-0.29
	(0.01)	(4.51)**	(-1.29)
14 Other manufacturing	-0.17	-0.72	0.45
20, 25, 36,37	(-0.79)	(2.09)**	(1.89)*
19 Wholesale, vehicle sales & repairs	-0.02	-0.46	0.68
50, 51	(-0.09)	(-1.03)	(2.46)**
Non-manufacturing	0.84	0.60	0.99
	(3.91)**	(3.11)**	(4.11)**
15 Electrical supply 40.1	0.22	0.81	-0.54
	(-0.89)	(-3.01)**	(-2.98)**
16 Gas Supply 40.2, 40.3	-0.17	-0.38	0.61
	(-0.89)	(-0.56)	(1.18)
17 Water supply 41	-0.26	-0.62	0.34
	(-1.12)	(-2.58)**	(1.39)
18 Construction 45	-0.05	0.98	-0.46
	(-0.27)	(5.15)**	(-1.80)*
20 Retailing 52	-0.16	0.94	-0.68
	(-0.83)	(1.26)	(-0.97)
21 Hotels & catering 55	-0.12	-0.14	-0.50
	(-0.57)	(-0.29)	(-1.69)*
22 Rail transport 60.1	-0.79	-0.92	-0.77
	(-3.89)**	(-1.31)	(-1.69)*
23 Road transport 60.2, 60.3	-0.31	-0.99	0.49
	(-1.70)*	(-5.28)**	(2.17)**
24 Water transport 61	0.56	0.99	-0.23
	(2.78)**	(5.18)**	(-0.71)
25 Air transport 62	-0.08	-0.99	0.36
	(-0.39)	(-5.26)**	(1.63)

26 Other transport services 63	-0.26	-0.99	0.60
	(-1.26)	(-4.95)**	(2.70)**
27 Communications 64	-0.06	0.97	-0.62
	(-0.27)	(4.66)**	(-2.71)**
28 Finance 65, 66	0.07	0.95	-0.52
	(0.37)	(5.86)**	(-1.96)**
29 Business services 67, 70, 71, 72, 73, 74	-0.35	-0.70	-0.31
	(-1.60)	(-3.46)**	(-0.95)
33 Waste treatment 90	-0.00	-0.93	0.62
	(-0.01)	(-1.57)	(1.53)
34 Miscellaneous services 91-99	0.25	-0.99	0.73
	(1.24)	(-5.03)**	(3.32)**

The level of significance is denoted by the asterisks (*) & (**) at 10% and 5% respectively. The U.K private economy

Table 5.4.3 BFK LABQA

SIC Industry	$cor(\Delta t, \Delta n)$	$cor(\Delta t, \Delta n / \varepsilon^z)$	$cor(\Delta t, \Delta n / \varepsilon^m)$
Aggregate manufacturing	0.73	0.44	0.97
	(3.84)**	(2.62)**	(3.48)**
Nondurables	-0.20	-0.97	0.37
	(-1.11)	(-5.14)**	(1.70)*
2 Oil & Gas 11, 12	0.16	0.99	-0.62
	(0.80)	(1.43)	(-1.16)
3 Coal & other mining 10, 13,14	-0.14	-0.24	0.43
	(-0.65)	(-0.35)	(0.91)
4 Manufactured fuel 23	0.24	-0.58	-0.75
	(-1.26)	(-0.82)	(-1.02)
5 Chemicals & pharmaceutical 24	0.15	0.99	-0.62
	(0.73)	(5.08)**	(-2.58)**
11 Food, drink & tobacco 15, 16	-0.26	-0.97	0.74
	(-1.27)	(-4.83)**	(3.60)**
12 Textiles, clothing & leather 17, 18, 19	0.75	0.30	0.97
	(3.69)**	(0.64)	(3.02)**
13 Paper, printing & publishing 21, 22	-0.38	0.47	-0.47
	(-1.89)*	(2.46)**	(-1.89)*

Durables	-0.19	-0.33	-0.42
	(-0.99)	(-1.01)	(-1.84)*
6 non-metallic mineral products	-0.32	-0.85	0.48
26	(-1.57)	(-4.83)**	(1.68)*
7 Basic metals & metal goods	0.16	0.94	-0.44
27, 28	(0.79)	(5.28)**	(-1.50)
8 Mechanical engineering 29	-0.54	-0.69	-0.52
	(-2.55)**	(-3.48)**	(-1.77)*
9 Electrical engineering &	-0.17	-0.79	0.45
electronics	(-0.88)	(-1.09)	(0.94)
30, 31, 32, 33	0.00	0.85	-0.31
10 Vehicles 34, 35	(0.02)	(4.84)**	(-1.36)
	-0.14	-0.62	0.47
14 Other manufacturing	(-0.70)	(-1.31)	(1.58)
20, 25, 36,37	0.00	-0.43	0.62
19 Wholesale, vehicle sales &	(0.00)	(-1.30)	(3.38)**
repairs			
50, 51			
Non-manufacturing	0.74	0.34	0.94
	(3.72)**	(0.47)	(1.79)*
15 Electrical supply 40.1	0.24	0.84	-0.57
	(1.19)	(3.40)**	(-2.78)**
16 Gas Supply 40.2, 40.3	-0.17	-0.39	0.61
	(-0.87)	(-0.55)	(1.11)
17 Water supply 41	-0.24	-0.62	0.38
	(-1.18)	(-2.29)**	(1.82)*
18 Construction 45	-0.09	0.99	-0.48
	(-0.41)	(4.84)**	(-1.81)*
20 Retailing 52	-0.13	0.98	- 0.74
	(-0.64)	(2.83)**	(-3.53)**
21 Hotels & catering 55	-0.13	-0.05	-0.53
	(-0.65)	(-0.14)	(-2.18)
22 Rail transport 60.1	-0.99	-0.99	- 0.99
	(-4.76)***	(-1.44)	(-2.09)*
23 Road transport 60.2, 60.3	-0.30	-0.99	0.50
	(-1.45)	(-4.79)**	(2.03)**
24 Water transport 61	0.58	0.99	-0.21
	(3.06)**	(5.37)**	(-0.67)

25 Air transport 62	-0.07	-0.99	0.35
	(-0.38)	(-5.61)**	(1.46)
26 Other transport services 63	-0.26	-0.99	0.59
	(-1.29)	(-5.30)**	(3.18)**
27 Communications 64	0.01	0.99	-0.66
	(0.06)	(5.69)**	(-2.55)**
28 Finance 65, 66	0.05	0.98	-0.58
	(0.26)	(5.28)**	(-2.38)**
29 Business services	-0.60	-0.21	-0.63
67, 70, 71, 72, 73, 74	(-3.04)**	(-1.14)	(-1.98)**
33 Waste treatment 90	0.00	-0.55	0.59
	(0.02)	(-0.88)	(1.35)
34 Miscellaneous services 91-99	0.31	-0.95	0.71
	(1.57)	(-5.08)**	(3.02)**

Data source: The data used in these estimations are the BEID. SIC92 is the 1992 version of the U.K.'s Standard Industrial Classification, which is identical to the European NACE system. The unconditional correlation estimate is column 1. The conditional correlation estimates are decomposition into technology and nontechnology shocks both for the TFP denoted as Δt and labor hours or employment as Δn respectively, columns 2 & 3. The level of significance is denoted by the asterisks (*) & (**) at 10% and 5% respectively. The terms z and m denotes technology and non-technology shocks. The table is for the U.K private business economy.

The result on the short run or unconditional correlation estimates in tables 5.3.1 to 5.3.3 TFP-hours shows similar pattern to that of long run or conditional correlations. In all, there is no evidence of contractionary effects on hours. The aggregate and disaggregate sectors had strong positive correlations. The only sectors on the nondurable manufacturing with strong positive correlations are: (3) Coal and other mining, (5) Chemicals and pharmaceutical, (11) Food, drink and tobacco, and (13) Paper, printing and publishing. The rest SIC's (2) Oil and Gas, (4) Manufactured fuel and (12) Textiles, clothing and leather all show negative hours or contractionary effects. For durable sectors TFP/

Hours, only Electrical engineering and electronics have a negative hours of -0.50 (-1.77) significant at 10% level. For non-manufacturing, the following sectors indicate a decline in hours after a positive technology shocks. (15) Electrical supply -0.67 (-1.30), (17) Water supply -0.69 (-1.29), (21) Hotels and catering -0.79 (-1.05), (23) Road transport -0.58 (-1.15), (24) Water transport -0.75 (-1.31), (26) Other transport services -0.79 (-2.66) significant at 5% level, (33) Waste treatment sector -0.69 (-1.01) and (34) Miscellaneous services sector -0.73 (-1.05). The rest of the sectors are positive.

5.6   The Sticky Price Issue

Let us now take a brief look at the policy implications on the issue of associations with sticky prices. I discussed in detail in chapter 4, the Sticky Price Model and the New Keynesian Economics (see the appendix). Hence, a full discussion is not necessary here. The reason for its consideration is that, the manufacturing sector VARs according to Chang et al (2006) exhibits some elements of heterogeneity in the response of hours (employment) to technology. In addition, a negative impulse response would imply inconsistency with the predictions of the underlying flexible price model (see the research questions). For example, Jermann (1998) indicate that with adjustment costs to investment, RBC models with flexible prices may show a negative response of hours to technology. Equally, Gali (1999) suggested a sticky price model as a mechanism to generate a negative effect of technology on employment. This is through examining employment's negative short run response to a permanent labor productivity shock in OECD countries.

What this means is that, it is easy to infer that when prices are fixed, the demand for goods and services will remain unchanged. Also at the same time, firms will require less input of labor to produce the same level of output because of improved efficiency. Further more, Dotsey (2002) and Gali, Lopez - Salido and Valles (2003) indicate that technology's impact on employment can as well depend on monetary policy. In other words, employment is capable of rising under the sticky price model if the government and/or the central bank, that is, the monetary authority, can actively adjust to technology shocks. See also CEV (2004) for a study on US and Canada, and Alves et al (2006) for the Banco Portugal study.

Further more, Chang et al (2006) examine whether industry's response of hours to technology shocks correlates with the stickiness of industry – output prices for the US. To do this, they adopted Bils and Klenow (2004) study, and compute the average-price change frequency, which is then match with the price quotes produced by the Bureau of Labor Statistics (BLS) for the period 1995 – 1997. In addition, they normalize technology shocks across industries. This is due to the assumption industries may have had different degrees of technological change over time. Hence, under sticky price hypothesis, they expect to find a negative correlation between the short run responses of hours worked and average price duration, but their study finds no systematic relationship. In addition, under a long run bivariate VAR of labor productivity growth and hours growth, they found no evidence of strong correlation between the responses of hours worked and the average duration of prices. They conclude that a low correlation indicates that price stickiness may not be a primary reason why firms employ hours differently when confronted with technological progress. Moreover, if there are no inventories, price stickiness should generate contractionary effects in response to technology shocks.

5.7 Labor Productivity and TFP Growth Shocks

In this section, the idea is to use labor productivity growth in place of TFP. This is because of the view that TFP is a more natural measure of technology as labor productivity reflects input mix as well as efficiency[59].

---

[59] See Chang and Hong (2006), American Economic Review, vol. 96 (1), p352 – 368.

Hence, I used the sectors shocks estimated using BFK, (2004) approach. In chapters 2 – 4, the concentration was on aggregate level estimations. In this chapter, the emphasis is on sectors. Equally, Kiley (1998) found the permanent components of labor productivity and employment negatively correlated in 15 two digit-manufacturing industries. Chang et al (2006) also reports a negative response of hours worked when labor productivity growth replaces TFP in a bivariate VAR. In this study, I show the results for the correlations in table 5.4. The results show no negative correlation when TFP is replaced by productivity (BFK) on aggregate level, except when estimated using hours (labqa)[60] on aggregate nondurables unconditional -0.20 (-1.11) and conditional technology -0.97 (-5.14), which is significant at 5 percent level. The parenthesis in brackets is the t-statistics. The aggregate durable sectors were negative but not significant. For unconditional it is -0.19 (-0.99) and for conditional it is -0.33 (-1.01) and -0.42 (-1.84) respectively.

On sector by sector for durable manufacturing, only mechanical engineering sector has hours worked negatively correlated with productivity growth, the unconditional bivariate estimate is -0.54 (-2.55), significant at 5% level, and for conditional bivariate estimate, it is -0.69 (-3.48) at 5% and -0.52 (1.77) at 10% significance level.. The SIC (19) Wholesale, vehicle sales and repairs sector has negative correlation on conditional technology shock of -0.43 (-1.30) and a strong (positive) hours increase of 0.62 (3.38) significant at 5% level (table 5.4.3). The nondurable sectors, on sectoral level for SIC (13) Paper, printing and publishing on short run or unconditional impact, has a decline of -0.38 (-1.89), which is significant at 10% level. For the long run or conditional (with restriction imposed), there is rise or positive impact effect of 0.47 (2.46) which is significant at 5% level while, hours decline by -0.47 (1.89) significant at 10%. It is similar result for Food, drink and tobacco. The unconditional bivariate is negative but insignificant -0.26 (-1.27).

---

[60] LABQA is total hours worked adjusted for quality, from the BEID (2003).

For the conditional bivariate estimate, technology is negative -0.97 (-4.83), while hours is positive 0.74 (3.60) both significant at 5% level respectively. In total, 4 out of 7 nondurable sectors had a decline on hour's worked and same numbers for durable sectors and 9 sectors for non-manufacturing sectors. For non-manufacturing in 7 sectors hours decline and significant at 5% level while, 3 sectors were positive at 5% level and 2 sectors show a rise in hours at 10% significant level. One sector, the SIC (18) Construction indicates a decline in hours of -0.48 (-1.81) significant at 10% level, with a positive technology shock of 0.99 (4.84) significant at 5% level. For the non-manufacturing on sectoral level, there is evidence of contractionary effects on hours or employment after a positive technology improvement following a technology shock based on these results.

Figure 5.2(a-d) displays the response to Cholesky one S.D Innovation ± 2 S.E of the shocks from the SVAR estimations using labor productivity instead of TFP. In comparison with the two approaches in estimations, there are some significant differences. In general, the TFP is more sensitive and robust than the labor productivity (tables 5.3.1 to 5.3.3 and 5.4.1 to 5.4.3 for the results respectively).

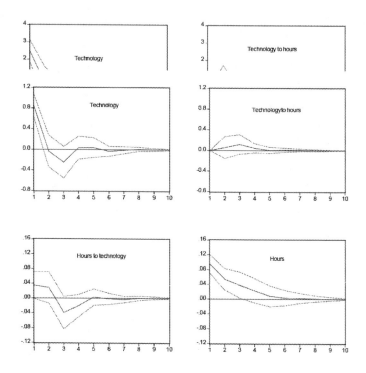

5.2B: Sector: Oil and Gas

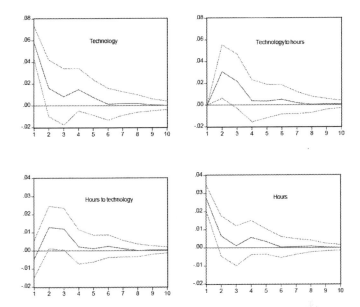

Figure 5.2: C: Other transport services sector

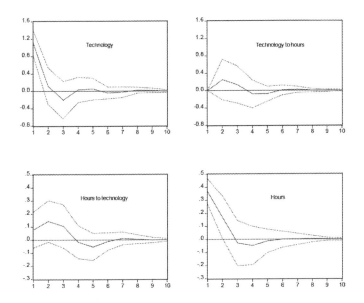

5.2D: Aggregate nondurable sectors

Finally, on aggregate level, there were no contractions. However, on sector by sector, some sectors had a negative impact. Hours responded strongly on the nondurable sector but decline more on the durable sector. On aggregate level, technology shock response is 0.44 (2.62) significant at 5% level and a strong positive increase of 0.97 (3.48) significant at 5% level for hours. I show these on figures 5.2 a-d above. At the sectoral level, TFP and labor productivity responds very differently. On nondurable sectors, some shocks affects TFP in long run than labor productivity. Equally, some shocks affect labor productivity more than TFP when focused on the durable sector. This could account for the increase use of outsourcing of intermediate products and services.

5.4   Conclusions

The evidence in this study indicates that technological innovations do lead to increase in employment in UK aggregate private business economy including manufacturing sectors. This implies a distinction in the study from those that found a negative impact or correlation between the permanent component of labor productivity and hours worked (employment) in manufacturing sectors. For example, a few studies for the US manufacturing found negative impacts between productivity and hours worked.

In chapter three of this study, our result shows only inputs has a negative sign on influence with a positive technology shocks. All the other variables tested in that chapter had a positive sign. In BFK (2004) when there is improvement in technology on impact input use declines. In addition, Gali found a negative response in hours to a positive technology, and the correlation between hours and productivity negative for technology shocks. There is no such evidence found in this study on aggregate level.

Given the econometric results with TFP in comparison with the labor productivity in this study, it may well be that TFP is the more appropriate natural measure for technology. TFP takes into account growth in aggregate output. To accommodate for welfare changes, this will involve removing the opportunity cost of the inputs used to produce the output growth. Further more, it is the input prices that measures the opportunity cost irrespective of whether they reflect marginal products or not. This is especially if productivity is different from technology. In which case, productivity most closely indexes welfare.

If we consider the results on sectoral or industry firm level, there is evidence of a contractionary effect in the UK manufacturing sectors, even though majority of these negative effects are statistically insignificant. Further more, it also depends on industry type for example, durable or non-durable manufacturing. The effects are not evenly distributed.

In Chang and Hong, (2006), their conclusion was that TFP is the natural measure for technology because labor productivity represents the input mix including technology. The distinction between TFP and productivity is evident from the results on the impact at sectoral level estimations, both from the structural VAR and from the regressions on current and lagged technology growth (table 5.2). Further more, the results in this chapter supports the findings in all the previous three substantive chapters of this book.

The research so far has been consistent in providing evidence of no contractionary effects on aggregate level for the UK manufacturing industries and/or the private economy sector (even though some industries exhibits it on sectoral level). In addition, when based on equation regressions on current and lagged TFP as well as labor productivity, the results are very similar to those from the SVAR model estimations.

Equally, the research has provided some evidence of contractionary effects for the whole UK (34 sectors) economy, ONS data based on the results in chapter 4 of book. The results in this chapter are on the UK private business economy, which has fewer sectors (30 sectors), BEID dataset in comparison with the whole UK economy analysis and as such answers the research question on contraction and conformity with the RBC theory predictions.

Appendix

A5.1 Econometric Tests: Endogeneity

The reason for this appendix is the correction for endogeneity in some of the regression estimations. Equally, in modelling for the TFP estimates, it uses fixed effect model. The measurement for TFP also includes using 2SLS, 3SLS and instrumental variables (IV). Hence, judging from the complexities of the modelling procedures in the book, providing this appendix is invaluable.

The term Endogeneity refers to the value of one independent variable being dependent on the value of other predictor variables. Because of this endogeneity, a significant correlation can exist between the unobserved factors contributing to both the endogenous independent variable and the dependent variable, thereby resulting to biased estimators. The correlation between the dependent variables can create substantial multicollinearity, which violates the assumptions of standard regression models and result to inefficient estimators.

This problem surfaces when models generate coefficient standard errors that are larger than true standard errors. This biases the interpretation towards the null hypothesis and increases the likelihood of a type II error. Thus, the power of the test of significance for an independent variable X_1 is reduced by a factor of $(1 - r^2_{(1/2,3....)})$, where $r_{(1/2,3,...)}$ is defined as the multiple correlation coefficient for the model

$X_1 = f(X_2, X_3....)$ and all X_i are independent variables in the larger model.

The specification for endogeneity and exogeneity are essential elements in the process of model specification, for example, a stochastic model (rather than a deterministic model). A deterministic model specifies for restriction requirements satisfaction by a vector of variable y. The restriction usually includes a second vector of variables x. The restrictions may only hold if x satisfies certain restrictions[61]. The model asserts:

$$\forall x \in R, \ G(x, y) = 0$$

Where: x is exogenous and the variable y is endogenous. The defining difference between x and y is that y may be (and is generally) restricted by x, but not conversely. For example, $\forall x \in R^1$, and $x + y = 0$. The condition $x + y = 0$ is symmetric in x and y. The stipulation is that x is exogenous and y is endogenously specified such that in the model x restricts y and not conversely. A major assumption of OLS regression is that the x_i values are uncorrelated with the error terms[62]. Let us use the following model as an example:

$$y_i = \beta_0 + \beta_1 x_i + \varepsilon_i \tag{A5.1}$$

The issue now is finding out what brings about this problem. The most frequent assumption is to view the problem as arising from an **Omitted Variable Bias (OVB).** This is the most commonly illustration of endogeneity. In other words, it implies that there is another variable which correlates with both x, and y so that after fitting the model above there are still a relationship with this other variable and the residuals.

Thus, the perception OVB poses the major difficulty on observational data. This is because of the interest to know whether the model above represents a causal relationship **(Causality)** between x and y or not. In other words, it implies that if we can manipulate x by raising one unit

---

[61] The New Palgrave Econometrics, edited by John Eatwell, Murray Milgate and Peter Newman, (1990), p75.

[62] This is impossible to confirm because only estimates of the error terms are available and if correlation exists, then these estimates will be incorrect.

of it, then y would increase by β_1 unit as well. In other words, this is just a **causal argument.**

The exogenous variables on the other hand, represent external shocks to the system. The other important source of endogeneity is **Reverse Causality.** Making a causal claim requires a truly exogenous variable. In other words, it requires a variable without a relation to any of the other variables in the system, observed and unobserved. The problem with observational data as in this research is that there are an infinite number of unobserved variables, which could render our observed relationship endogenous. This is the problem of unobserved heterogeneity in our sample.

To tackle the problem, we consider the following basic format:

1. To make an argument about how and why things are as they are.
2. To show the available empirical data are consistent with our argument.
3. To demonstrate that the available empirical data are inconsistent with counter-arguments for how and why things are as they are.

The third scenario in the basic format above is the pivotal one. No method can perfectly recover causality from observational data, but in some cases, it can effectively reduce the range of plausible counter-stories. Hence, I consider in this case, the two most common methods frequently adopted for solutions.

A5.2.1: The Fixed Effect Models

The first solution approach is the fixed effect models. This comes primarily from longitudinal data designs in which there are repeated observations on an individual over time. They can apply more broadly. An example in this case would be to use equation (1) and control for any observed variables that may be confounding the relationship. In that respect, we can obtain the following the expression:

$$y_{it} = \beta_0 + \beta_1 s_{it} + \lambda x_{it} + \gamma z_i \varepsilon_{it} \tag{A5.2}$$

Where y is hours, s_{it} is the technology, x_{it} is the observed time varying for firm i in period t and z_i is a set of time constant unobserved variable for firm i. The model estimates the average difference between hours and technology with β_1, controlling for all observed time varying constant covariates and ε_{it} the error term or white noise.

This model is problematic because it does not take into account that there are repeated observations on the same firms, which can lead to correlated error terms within the firms. To deal with this therefore, we can utilize the longitudinal design to eliminate some of the unobserved heterogeneity (and to correct the issue with error terms). The first task is to define a set of dummy terms, D_i and assign the value of one if the observation comes from individual i and zero if otherwise. Adding these dummy terms to the model would yield the following expression:

$$y_{it} = \beta_0 + \beta_1 s_{it} + \lambda x_{it} + \alpha_1 D_i + \varepsilon_{1t} \tag{A5.3}$$

or

$$y_{it} = \beta_0 + \beta_1 s_{it} + \lambda x_{it} + \alpha_1 + \varepsilon_{1t} \tag{A5.4}$$

The dummy variables permits for a term to be fitted for every individual. The α term is the **fixed effects**. In addition, there is no need to include the observed z_i terms in the model. This is because the term D_i explains all the time constant variations across individuals, so that they supersede the term z_i. In other words, we would have a reduced form equation as:

$$\alpha_i = \gamma_1 z_i + \gamma_2 z_i^{U} \tag{A5.5}$$

The equation (A5.5) implies that, the fixed effects can account for both observed and unobserved time constant variables.

A5.2.2: The Instrumental Variables Model

The second solution approach is the instrumental variables. The basic relationship is equation (1). Since x_i might be endogenous we cannot trust our estimate of β_1. Therefore, we can obtain an instrumental variables estimate of β_1 as:

$$b_1^{IV} = \frac{Cov(y,z)}{Cov(x,z)} = \frac{Cov(\beta_0 + \beta_1 x + \varepsilon, z)}{Cov(x,z)} = \frac{Cov(x,z)\beta_1 + Cov(\varepsilon,z)}{Cov(x,z)} \tag{A5.6}$$

If the assumption is correct about the instrument z, then $Cov(\varepsilon, z) = 0$, and hence:

$$b_1^{IV} = \frac{Cov(x,z)\beta_1 + Cov(\varepsilon,z)}{Cov(x,z)} = \frac{Cov(x,z)\beta_1}{Cov(x,z)} = \beta \tag{A5.7}$$

Therefore, the IV estimator will be an unbiased estimator of β_1. The effect of this is that we have used the exogenous shock of the instrument to clean out any endogenous relationship between x and y.

The two-stage least squares (2SLS) is the most common method of doing the actual estimation. Note that our estimations for the TFP in the text also made use of 2SLS regression method. Therefore, the first step is to predict the value of x_i and z_i. Other terms to this final model for y, can be included as ω_i,

$$\hat{x}_i = \alpha_0 + \alpha_1 x_i + \alpha_2 \omega_i \qquad\qquad (A5.8)$$

The second step is to use the predicted value of x rather than its real value in an OLS regression predicting y:

$$y_i = \beta_0 + \beta_1 \hat{x}_i + \beta_2 \omega_i + \varepsilon_i \qquad\qquad (A5.9)$$

Utilising the predicted value of x will imply leaving aside the residuals from the first equation. More over, given that z is an exogenous shock on x, the residuals are in a sense part of x, which are potentially endogenous with y. This method effectively strips it away. These varying views tend to be esoteric and as such, the value of the IV approach becomes questionable. Ideally, using IV should be where the endogeneity of x is clear and irresolvable. Thus, using IV should be a complement to rather than a substitute for OLS.

A5.3: The Testing For Endogeneity Methodology

We consider here the methodological approaches used to test for endogeneity in the regression estimates. The 2SLS estimators are usually regard as not being on the same par as OLS estimators. According to Wooldridge (2003), 2SLS estimator is less efficient than OLS when the explanatory variables are exogenous. Since 2SLS estimators can have very large standard errors, it is useful to test for endogeneity of an explanatory variable to determine whether 2SLS is necessary.

Therefore, if we assume that there is a single suspected endogenous variable of the form:

$$y_1 = \beta_0 + \beta_1 y_2 + \beta_2 \tau_1 + \beta_3 \tau_2 + u_1 \qquad\qquad (A5.10)$$

Where τ_1 and τ_2 are exogenous. Furthermore, assume there are two additional exogenous variables τ_3 and τ_4 not shown in equation (A5.10). If y_2 is uncorrelated with u_1, then it is possible to estimate equation (A5.10) by OLS.

A5.3.1: The Testing Approach

A simplistic method on how to test for endogeneity is to use the Hausman (1978) suggestion. The suggestion was to compare the OLS and 2SLS estimates, and then determine if the differences are statistically significant. Both the OLS and the 2SLS are consistent if all the variables are exogenous. If the 2SLS and the OLS differ significantly, then y_2 must be endogenous and implies that τ_j must be exogenous. To determine if the differences are statistically significant, it is easier to use a regression test. This is on estimating the reduced form for y_2 which is:

$$y_2 = \pi_0 + \pi_1\tau_1 + \pi_2\tau_2 + \pi_3\tau_3 + \pi_4\tau_4 + v_2 \qquad (A5.11)$$

Since each τ_j is uncorrelated with u_1, y_2 is uncorrelated with u_1 if and only if v_2 is uncorrelated with u_1. In other words, we wish to test: $u_1 = \delta_1 v_2 + e_1$ where e_1 is uncorrelated with v_2 and has a zero mean. Therefore, v_2 are uncorrelated if and only if $\delta_1 = 0$. In testing for this, we have to include v_2 as an additional regressor in equation (A5.10) and to do a t – test. There is only one problem with implementing this and that is, v_2 is not observed, because it is an error term in equation (A5.11). Since we can estimate the reduced form for y_2 by OLS, we can therefore obtain the reduced form residual $\hat{v}_2$. Hence, we estimate:

$$y_1 = \beta_0 + \beta_1 y_2 + \beta_2\tau_1 + \beta_3\tau_2 + \delta_1\hat{v}_2 + error \qquad (A5.12)$$

Using OLS estimation: and test (the null) $H_0 : \delta_1 = 0$ using a t statistic. If we reject H_0 at a small significance level, then y_2 is endogenous because v_2 and u_1 are correlated.

A5.3.2 Testing for Endogeneity of a Single Explanatory Variable

1. The first step is to estimate the reduced form for y_2 by regressing it on all exogenous variables, including those in the structural equation and the additional IVs. This enables us to obtain the residual $\hat{v}_2$.

2. The second step is to add $\hat{v}_2$ to the structural equation, which includes y_2 and test for the significance of $\hat{v}_2$ using an OLS regression. If the coefficient on $\hat{v}_2$ is statistically different from zero, then y_2 is indeed endogenous. To check for robust t test, we can use a heteroskedasticity test.

An interesting feature of the regression from step (2) is that the estimates on all of the variables, except $\hat{v}_2$ are identical to the 2SLS estimates. For example, by estimating equation (A5.12) by OLS gives $\hat{\beta}_j$ that is identical to the 2SLS estimates from equation (A5.10). This is a simple way to ensure doing proper regression for endogeneity. It also gives another interpretation of 2SLS including $\hat{v}_2$ in the OLS regression equation (A5.12) clears up the endogeneity of y_2.

Furthermore, we can also test for endogeneity of multiple explanatory variables. For each suspected endogenous variable, we obtain the reduced form residuals as in step (1) above. Then we test for joint significance of these residuals in the structural equation, using an F test. Joint significance indicates that at least one suspected explanatory variable is endogenous. The number of exclusion restrictions tested is the number of suspected endogenous explanatory variables.

Notes & Discussions

Notes & Discussions

Chapter 6

Concluding Remarks

In this chapter, I present the overall conclusions drawn from the research and a summary from the five substantive chapters of this book. This concluding chapter structure is as follows: in section, 6.1 are the empirical research findings while in section 6.2 are the summaries and concluding remarks.

6.1: The Empirical Research Findings

Most research studies concerning the response of hours concentrated solely on the estimation approach and paid little attention to the sources other than what happens after a positive technology shocks, that is, technology or nontechnology. This book aims to shed some light on the response source issue through the decomposition of technology. To arrive at these findings, employing econometrics-modelling techniques to test, establish and enhance on the methodological approaches was necessary. An example of this is the use of direct measure of technology and the structural vector autogressive (SVAR) model. As a departure from the usual real business cycle (RBC) model calibration and simulation approach, the econometrics modelling made use of time series data of the economy. This research also confirms the importance of controlling for imperfect competition to measure accurately, aggregate productivity and aggregate technology, hence answering questions 1 and 2 of the research questions.

In this book I investigated the different advocated techniques in measuring the response of hours following a positive technology shocks. Depending on the empirical estimation approach and definition of hours worked, the research did not find significant evidence of contractionary effect within the UK private business economy at aggregate level. On the sectoral level, only few sectors showed evidence of contractionary effects and most of them are insignificant. When applied to the UK manufacturing sectors using a direct measure of technology, there is no evidence of contractionary effects found at aggregate level. In this respect, technology drives productivity and hours worked up, hence, making it possible to conclude that the model is consistent with the RBC model predictions. This answers two of the key research questions (3 and 4) in chapter 1.

Further more, in terms of the difference between aggregate productivity and aggregate technology, the distinction between them is due to increases in efficiency and/or improvements in technology. This answers the research question 1.

In terms of the results reported in this book, it affirms controlling for imperfect competition importance, thus answering again the research question 2. This is because of the sectoral markups and reallocations of resources. Another possible interpretation of the empirical results is that it confirms the importance of permanent improvement in the economy given the productivity level performance over technology. This manifests to a higher level of output distribution and consumption without causing any changes in technology. The postulation is that aggregate productivity and aggregate technology are responsible for the welfare improvement. The impulse that is driving productivity and hours up is the technology. This again answers the research questions 1 and 2.

The empirical result from chapter 3 shows that technology innovations do not contract input use and therefore answers the research question 3.

The evidence from chapter 4 shows that hours worked fall or rise after a positive permanent technology shock depending on the treatment of hours. There is a clear evidence of contraction following the method advocated by Gali (1999) and as such answers the research question 3.

The evidence from chapter 5 indicates that technological innovations do lead to increase in employment in the U.K. aggregate private business economy including the manufacturing sector and therefore answer the research question 4.

Currently there is no consensus on a definitive methodology for universal adoption by economists. It is not clear if a harmonized model is feasible as shown in tables 1.0 and 1.2 of chapter 1. This study has examined the various methodologies advocated in the literatures. It has contributed in providing a platform upon which future research for improvement can be undertaken. As shown in this book, the estimation of the response of hours or employment after a positive technology shock depends to a certain extent on the treatment of hours, as well as on the definition of hours worked itself. The book has contributed to clarify some of these definition and/or, empirical problems associated with hours worked and the possible influence over the outcome.

6.2   Summary Conclusions

The findings in this study have answered all our research questions as hypothesised in chapter 1. Therefore, it is feasible to observe:

1) The relationship between aggregate productivity and aggregate technology, and has contributed in presenting an enhanced understanding of the impact of TFP on employment.
2) It has made it possible to obtain a better picture for example, the U.K disaggregate manufacturing industries in terms of productivity and employment.

Through the literature review, I conducted a comprehensive examination of various hypothesis and findings by other studies. This process provided a further insight to TFP and RBC theories, for example, seminal studies by Kydland and Prescott (1982), Lucas (1977, 1980), Long and Plosser (1983), Cooley (1995), King and Rebelo (2000), Gali (1999), Basu and Fernald (2002), and Basu, Fernald and Kimball (2004).

In addition to the RBC, the book also reviewed the economic growth theory of the neoclassical and endogenous growth models. The two models are important and relevant to the study in that, for example, Solow (1957), and Lucas (1975), made use of the neoclassical growth theory. Since the estimation of TFP is crucial in this book, examining the two economic growth theories is imperative.

The neoclassical and endogenous models have different assumptions in relation to technology in the production function. Given the production function used in this study, I therefore in chapters 4 and 5, decomposed technology in order to identify the sources of technology. The identification process of technology in this book is very important, especially given the predictions of RBC models.

Chapter 2 provided the model specification at aggregate level and as such form the first substantive empirical chapter of the book. The chapter also shows the distinction between aggregate productivity and aggregate technology. The chapter show the pivotal role of markups in estimating aggregate productivity and aggregate technology, implying the need to control for imperfect competition.

The estimations in chapters 3, 4 and 5 used purified technology as a proxy. At disaggregate level, the natural measure of firms output is the gross output. In the BFK (2004) model, when technology improves, upon impact input use falls while output changes very marginally. Equally, Gali (1999), Kiley (1998), Francis and Ramey (2002) all show results with a reduction in total hours worked.

The results in this study showed a rise in total hours, which is in line with the RBC, models prediction. Shea (1999) also found an increase in input use especially labor in the short run. Further more, in Chang and Hong (2006), the effect on hours varied across industries, with some showing a reduction and others indicating a rise in hours. The chapter draws attentions to the policy implications of the findings, especially in relation to monetary policy. It is essential for the authorities to determine how to react to technology shocks in order to adjust to new level of full employment output.

Chapter 4 on the other hand concentrated on SVAR model in estimating technology shocks and aggregate fluctuations. The results shows that total hours worked fall or rise after a positive permanent technology shocks depending on the treatment of hours. It also showed a strong positive co-movement between technology and hours.

Following the proposed methodology, there is some evidence of contractionary effects in the UK manufacturing sectors, even though majority of these negative effects are statistically insignificant. However, there is no evidence of contraction for the UK using direct measure of technology. Finally, chapter 5 dealt with the effect of technological innovations in the economy, especially in determining whether it increases or reduces the level of employment that is, contractionary effect.

The methodological approach adopted in chapter 5 examines the effects on UK private economy, identified by the permanent components of industry's TFP increases or for evidence of contractionary effects on hours or employment. Evidence from VAR model of the UK private economy sectors for the period 1970 – 2000 shows the effect of technology on employment to vary significantly across sectors on sectoral or disaggregate level. Equally, a good proportion of the sectors indicate a temporary reduction in employment in response to a permanent increase or reduction in TFP. In addition, many sectors exhibits increases in both employment and hours per worker in the short run. The results in this study confirm and/ or are in line with those of Chang and Hong (2006) for the US manufacturing industries (1958 – 1996).

In terms of the contribution of this book, the results in the study indicate that technological innovations do lead to increase in employment within the aggregate private business economy, for example the U.K economy. Equally, it implies a distinction in the study from those that found a negative impact or correlation between the permanent component of labor productivity and hours worked in the manufacturing sector. In addition, given the econometric modelling results with TFP in comparison with the labor productivity in this study, therefore, we can assume that TFP is perhaps the appropriate natural measure for technology. This is because labor productivity represents the input mix including technology. In addition, the difference between TFP and Productivity is evident from the results on impact at disaggregate sectoral levels, both from the SVAR and the lagged technology growth.

Notes & Discussions

Notes & Discussions

Bibliography

Aghion, P and Howitt, P (1998), "Endogenous Growth Theory", MIT Press Cambridge

Agiakoglou, C. and P. Newbold (1992), "Empirical evidence on Dickey-Fuller type tests," Journal of Time Series Analysis, 13, 471 – 483.

Alexius, A., and M. Carlsson (2001), "Measures of technology and the business cycle: evidence from Sweden and the U.S", FIEF working paper series, No.174, 1-47; and The Review of Economics and Statistics, May 2005, 87(2): 299-307

Alves, N., J. B. de Brito., S. Gomes, J. Sousa (2006), 'The effects of a technology shock in the Euro area', Banco de Portugal Economic Research Department WP 1-06, 1-24

Albergaria de Magalhaes, M., (2005), "Is the Solow residual a good proxy for technology shocks? Evidence for the Brazilian industry", VIII Encontro de Economia da Regiao Sul – ANPEC SUL 2005, 1 – 19

Altig, D; Christiano, L.J; Eichenbaum, M and Linde, J; (2002), "Technology Shocks and Aggregate fluctuations (Preliminary and Incomplete)", June 30, 2002, Manuscript

Anyalezu, N.K.G., (2014), "An Analysis of the Empirical Modelling Approaches to the Real Business Cycle (RBC) Model and Aggregate Technology", International Journal of Business, Humanities and Technology, Vol. 4 No. 1, January (2014) 60 – 72

Anyalezu, N.K.G., (2013), "Theory Analysis of Total Factor Productivity, Real Business Cycle Model and Economic Policy", International Journal of Business, Humanities and Technology, Vol. 3 No. 6, June (2013) 8 - 18

Anyalezu, N.K.G., (2011), "The Aggregate Technology and Contractionary Effects: An Empirical Estimation", International Business & Economics Research Journal, Volume 10, Number 7, July (2011), 47 – 66.

Arrow, K.J (1962), "The Economic Implications of Learning by Doing", Review of Economic Studies, 39, 155-173.

Baily, M.N., Hulten, C., Campbell, D., (1992), "Productivity dynamics in manufacturing plants", Brookings Papers on Economic Activity (Microeconomics) 1, 187 – 267

Banerjee, A and Russell, B (2004), "A reinvestigation of the Markup and the business cycle", Economic Modelling 21, (2004) 267 – 284

- (2002), "Inflation and measures of the markup", European University Institute Working Paper, ECO No. 2002/15

Banerjee, A; Cockerell, L and Russell, B (2001), An I (2) analysis of inflation and the markup, Sargan special issue, Journal of Applied Economics 16, 221 – 240

Bai, C.E., Li, D.D., and Wang, Y., 1997, "Enterprise productivity and efficiency: When is up really down"? Journal of Comparative Economics 24, 265 - 280

Barro, R and Becker, G (1989), "Fertility and Choice in a Model of Economic Growth", Econometrics 57, 481 – 501.

Barro, Robert J. and Sala-i-Martin, Xavier (1995), 'Economic growth' p16-17, McGraw-Hill

Basu, S., Fernald, J., and Kimball, M, 2004, "Are Technology Improvements Contractionary"? NBER Working Paper Series10592; - 1999, working paper, Chicago Federal Reserve

Basu, S and Fernald, J. G 2002 "Aggregate Productivity and Aggregate Technology", European Economic Review 46, 963 – 991

Basu, S and Fernald, J.G 1997b "Aggregate Productivity and Aggregate Technology", International Finance Discussion Paper no. 593, Board of Governors of the Federal Reserve System

Basu, S., (1995), "Intermediate goods and business cycles: Implications for productivity and welfare". American Economic Review 85, 512 – 531.

Basu, S., (1996), "Cyclical productivity: Increasing returns or cyclical utilisation"? Quarterly Journal of Economics 111, 719 – 751.

Basu, S., Fernald, J.G., (1997a), Returns to scale in U.S. manufacturing: Estimates and implications. Journal of Political Economy 105, 249 – 283.

Baxter, M and King, R.G., 1999, "Measuring Business cycles: Approximate Band-Pass Filters for Economic Time Series", The Review of Economics and Statistics, 81(4), 575-593

Berndt, E.R and Fuss, M.A., 1986, "Productivity measurement with adjustments for variations in capacity utilization and other forms of temporary equilibrium", Journal of Econometrics 33, 7 – 29

Bhargava, A. (1986), "On the Theory of Testing for Unit Roots in Observed Time Series," Review of Economic Studies, 53, 137 – 160

Bils, M. and Klenow, P. J. 2004, "Some Evidence of the Importance of Sticky Prices", Journal of Political Economy, 112(5), 947 – 85

Blanchard, O.J. (1989), "A traditional interpretation of macroeconomic fluctuations", the American Economic Review, Vol. 79, No. 5, 1146 – 1164

Blanchard, O. J., and Quah, D (1998), "The Dynamic Effects of Aggregate Demand and Supply Disturbances", the American Economic Review, vol. 79, No.4, 655-673

Braun, R.A. (1994), Tax Disturbances and Real Economic Activity in the Postwar United States", Journal of Monetary Economics, Vol.33, 441-462.

Burnside, C and Eichenbaum, M, 1996, "Factor-Hoarding and the Propagation of Business Cycle Shocks", the American Economic Review, Vol. 86, No.5, 1154 – 1174

Burnside, C; Eichenbaum, M and Rebelo, S, 1993, "Labour Hoarding and the Business Cycle", Journal of Political Economy, April 1993, Vol. 101, No. 2, 245 – 73.

Carlsson, M. 2003, "Measures of Technology and the Short run Response to Technology Shocks", Scandinavian Journal of Economics, 105(4), 555 – 579

Caves, D.W; Christensen, L.R; and Swanson, J.A (1981), "Productivity Growth, Scale Economies and Capacity Utilization in U.S. Railroads, 1955-74," The American Economic Review, Vol. 71, No.5 (Dec., 1981), 994-1002.

Caves, D.W; Christensen, L.R; and Swanson, J.A (1980), "Productivity in U.S. Railroads, 1951-1974", Bell Journal of Economics, Vol.11, No.1 (Spring 1980), 166-181.

Chamberlin, G. and Yueh, L. 2006, Macroeconomics, Thomson, London, 271 – 300

Chang, Y and Hong, J.H, 2006, "Do Technological Improvements in the Manufacturing Sector Raise or Lower Employment"? The American Economic Review, Vol. 96 No.1, 352 - 368

Chang, Y and Hong, J.H, 2006, "On the Employment Effect of Technology: Evidence from U.S. Manufacturing for 1958 – 1996", Federal Reserve Bank of Richmond Working Paper 03 – 06, 1-32

Christensen, L.R., and D.W. Jorgenson, "U.S. Real Product and Real Factor Input, 1929 – 1967," Review of Income and Wealth, Series 16 (1970), 19 – 50.

Christiano, L.J., and Eichenbaum, M, 1992, "Identification and the Liquidity Effect of a Monetary policy Shock", in Political Economy, Growth and Business Cycles, edited by Alex Cukierman, Zvi Hercowitz and Leonardo Leiderman, Cambridge and London: MIT Press, 335 - 370

Christiano, L.J., and Eichenbaum, M, (1992), "Liquidity Effect of a Monetary policy and the business cycle, NBER WP No. 4129, 1-41

Christiano, L.J., and Eichenbaum, M. (1992), "Current Real Business Cycle Theories and Aggregate Labour Market Fluctuations", the American Economic Review, Vol. 82, No. 3, 430-450.

Christiano, L. J., Eichenbaum, M and Vigfusson, R., 2004, "The Response of Hours to a Technology Shock: Evidence Based on Direct Measures of Technology", Journal of the European Economic Association, 2(2 – 3), 381 – 95

Christiano, L.J., Eichenbaum, M and Vigfusson, R., 2003, "What Happens After A Technology Shock"? NBER Working Paper 9819; Board of Governors of the Federal Reserve System, International Finance Discussion Paper, No. 768, June 2003, 1-52

Christiano, L.J., Eichenbaum, M and Vigfusson, R., 2003, "How do Canadian Hours Worked Respond to a Technology Shock?" Board of Governors of the Federal Reserve System, International Finance Discussion Paper, No. 774, September 2003, 1-20

Clarida, R., Gali, J., and Gertler, M., 2000, "Monetary Policy Rules and Macroeconomic Stability: Evidence and Some Theory", Quarterly Journal of Economics, 115, 147 – 180.

Cooley, T. F and Prescott, E .C, (1995), "Economic Growth and Business Cycles", in Thomas F Cooley, ed., Frontiers of Business Cycle Research Princeton, Princeton University Press

Cooley, T.F. and Hansen, G.D. (1989), "The Inflation Tax in a Real Business Cycle Model", the American Economic Review, Vol.7, No.4, 733-748.

Cooper, R.W. (1997), "Business Cycles: Theory, Evidence and Implications", NBER Working Paper, No.5994, 1-44.

Correia, I; Rabelo, S and Naves, J.C. (1995), "Business Cycles in a Small Open Economy", CEPR Discussion Paper No. 996.

DeJong, D.N., J.C. Nankervis, N.E. Savin, and C.H. Whiteman (1992a), "The power problems of unit root tests in time series with autoregressive errors," Journal of Econometrics, 53, 323-433.

Denison, Edward F., 1972, "Some Major Issues in Productivity Analysis: an Examination of the Estimates by Jorgenson and Griliches," Survey of current Business, 49 (5, Part II), 1 – 27

Denison, E.F.: "The Sources of Economic Growth in the United States and the Alternatives before Us," Supplementary Paper No. 13, Committee for Economic Development, New York, 1962

Dickey, D.A., D.P. Hasza, and W.A. Fuller (1984), "Testing for Unit Roots in Seasonal Time Series," Journal of American Statistical Association, 79, 355-367

Diewert, W.E., (1988), "The Early History of Price index Research", Working Paper No. 2713, National Bureau of Economic Research, Cambridge, Mass. 1-65.

Diamond, P.A., Mirrlees, J.A., (1971), "Optimal taxation and public production II: Tax rules". American Economic Review 61, 261 – 278.

Domar, E.D., 1961, "On the Measurement of Technical Change", Economic Journal 71, 710 – 729

Dotsey, M. 2002, "Structure from Shocks", Federal Reserve Bank of Richmond Economic Quarterly, 88(4), 37 – 47

Dougherty, C and D.W. Jorgenson, 1996, "International Comparisons of the Sources of Economic Growth", the American Economic Review", The American Economic Review, Vol. 86, Issue 2, Papers and Proceedings of the Hundredth and Eighth Annual Meeting of the American Economic Association San Francisco, CA, January 5-7, 1996 (May, 1996), 25 - 29

Elliott, G., T.J. Rothenberg, and J.H. Stock (1996), "Efficient Tests for an Autoregressive Unit Root," Econometrica, 64, 813-836.

Faust, J and E.M. Leeper, 1997, "When Do Long-run Identifying Restrictions Give Reliable Results?", American Statistical Association, Journal of Business and Economic Statistics, July 1997, Vol. 15, No. 3, 345 – 453

Farmer, R and Guo, J. T., 1994, "Real business Cycles and the Animal Spirits Hypothesis", Journal of Economic Theory 63, 42 - 72

Fisher, J., 2005, "The dynamic Effects of Neutral and Investment-Specific Shocks", Manuscript, Federal Reserve Bank of Chicago, 1 – 45

Fisher, J., 2006, "The dynamic Effects of Neutral and Investment-Specific Shocks", Journal of political Economy, Vol. 114, No. 3, 413 - 451

Franco, F and Philippon, T, 2004, "Firms and Aggregate Dynamics", this draft: April 2006; first draft: October 2004, mimeo, 1-38

Francis, N and Ramey, V. A, 2004, "A New Measure of Hours Per Capita with Implications for the Technology-Hours Debate" NBER, 1-32

Francis, N.R., Owyang, M.T., and Theodorou, A.T., 2005, "What Explains the Varying Monetary Response to Technology Shocks in

G-7 Countries", International Journal of Central Banking, Vol.1 No.3, 33 – 70

Francis, N.R, Owyang, M.T, and Theodorou, A.T (2003), "The use of long run restrictions for the identification of technology shocks", Federal Reserve Bank of St.Louis Review, 53 -65

Gali, J., 1999, "Technology, Employment and the Business Cycle: Do Technology Shocks Explain Aggregate Fluctuations"? American Economic Review 89, 249 – 271

Gali, J., Lopez-Salido, J.D., and Valles, J., 2003, "Technology Shocks and Monetary Policy: Assessing the Fed's Performance", Journal of Monetary Economics, 50(4), 723 – 43.

Gali, J., 2004, "On the Role of Technology Shocks as a Source of Business Cycles: Some New Evidence", Journal of the European Economic Association, Vol. 2(2 – 3), 372 – 380

Gali, J., (2005) "Trends in Hours, Balanced Growth, and the Role of Technology in the Business Cycle", Federal Reserve Bank of St. Louis Review, 87(4), 459-86.

Gali, J. and Rabanal, P., 2004, "Technology Shocks and Aggregate Fluctuations: How well does the RBC Model fit Postwar U.S. data", NBER Macroeconomics Annual, 2004, 2 – 66; IMF WP/04/234, 2004

Gordon, R. J. 2006, Macroeconomics, 10th edition, Pearson International Edition, London, 57 – 59

Granger, C.W.J (1969), "Investigating Causal Relations by Econometric Models and Cross-Spectral Methods", Econometrica, 37, 24-36.

Greenaway, D; Bleaney, M, and Stewart, I ((1996) editors), "A Guide to Modern Economics, Routledge London and New York

Griliches, Z. 1986, "Productivity Puzzles and R&D: another non explanation," Journal of Economic Perspectives, 2(4), 9-21.
Griliches, Z. 1994, "Explanations of Productivity Growth: Is the Glass half-empty?" American Economic Review, 84(1), 1-25.
Griliches, Z. 1979, "Issues in Assessing the Contribution of R&D to Productivity Growth", the Bell Journal of Economics, 10(1), 92-116
Griliches, Z. and Lichtenberg, F. 1984, "Inter-industry Technology Flows and Productivity Growth: A Re-examination". The Review of Economics and Statistics, Vol. 66, No.2. (May, 1984), 324-329

Hall, R. E and Jones, C.I., 1996, "The Productivity of Nations," NBER Working Paper Series 5812

Hall, R.E., 1988, "The relation between price and marginal cost in U.S. industry". Journal of Political Economy 96, 921 – 947.

Hall, R. E., 1973, "The specification of Technology with several kinds of output", JPE, volume 81, issue 4, p. 878-892

Hall, R.E., 1990, "Invariance properties of Solow's productivity residual". In: Diamond, P. (Ed.), Growth, Productivity, Employment. MIT Press, Cambridge, MA

Hansen, G.D. (1985), "Indivisible Labour and the Business Cycle", Journal of Monetary Economics, Vol. 16, 309-327.

Hartley, F.E., Hoover, K. D., Salyer, K. D., 1997, "The limits of business cycle research: Assessing the real business cycle model", Oxford Review of Economic Policy, vol. 13, no. 3, 34 – 54

Heijdra, B. J., and Van der Ploeg, F., 2002, Foundations of Modern Macroeconomics, Oxford University Press, 477 - 539

Horvath, M.T.K., 2000, "Sectoral Shocks and Aggregate Fluctuations", Journal of Monetary Economics 45, 69 – 106

Hoy, M., Livernois, J., Mckenna, C., Rees, R., and Stengos, T., (2001), 2nd ed., Mathematics for Economics. MIT Press, Camb. MA., pp. 23-66, 125-139,527 – 645, 660 – 63, 701-707

Hulten, C., (1978), "Growth accounting with intermediate inputs", Review of Economic Studies 45, 511 – 518

Hulten, C., 2000, "Total Factor Productivity: A Short Biography," NBER, Working Paper No. 7471

Hulten, Charles R, "Divisia Index Numbers," Econometrica, Vol. 41, No. 6 (Nov. 1973), 1017-1025.

Hulten, C and Srinivasan, S., 1999, "Indian Manufacturing Industry: Elephant or Tiger", Draft Paper, University of Maryland

Jermann, U. J., 1998, "Asset Pricing in Production Economies", Journal of Monetary Economics, 41(2), 257 – 275

Jones, C.I (1995), "R & D Based Models of Economic Growth", Journal of Political Economy, 103 (4): 759-784.

Jorgenson, D.W., 1990, "Aggregate Consumer Behaviour and the measurement of Social Welfare", Econometrica, Vol. 58, Issue 5, (Sep., 1990), 1007 – 1040

Jorgenson, D.W., Gollop, F., Fraumeni, B., (1987), "Productivity and U.S. Economic Growth", Harvard University Press, Cambridge, MA

Jorgenson, D.W. and Zvi Griliches, 1972, "Issues in Growth Accounting: A Reply to Edward F. Denison," Survey of Business, 52, 65 – 94

Jorgenson, D.W., and Z. Griliches: "The Explanation of Productivity Change," Review of Economic Studies, 34 (1967), 249-283.

Katz, L.F and Summers, L.H (1989), "Industry rents: Evidence and implications". Brookings Papers on Economic Activity (Microeconomics) (1), 209 – 290.

Kendrick, J (1961), "Productivity Trends in the United States," New York: National Bureau of Economic Research, 1961.

Khan, H and Tsoukalas, J (2006), "Technology Shocks and UK Business Cycles", first draft: April 2005, this draft: January 2006, mimeo 1-55

King, R.G., C.I. Plosser, J.H. Stock and M. Watson (1991), "Stochastic Trends and Economic Fluctuations", the American Economic Review, Vol. 81, No. 4, 819 - 840

King, R.G. and Plosser, C.I. (1984), "Money, Credit and Prices in a Real Business Cycle", the American Economic Review, Vol. 74, No.3, 363-380.

Koopmans, T.C (1965), "On the concept of Optimal Economical growth", in the Econometric Approach to Economic Planning, Amsterdam, North-Holland

Kwiatkowski D., P.C.B. Phillips, P. Schmidt, and Y. Shin (1992), "Testing the null Hypothesis of Stationary against the Alternative of a Unit Root," Journal of Econometrics, 54, 159-178.

Kydland, F. E. and Prescott, E. C., 1982, "Time to build and Aggregate Fluctuations", Econometrica, vol.50, No., 6, Nov., 1982, 1345 – 1370

Kydland, F. E. and Prescott, E. C., 1991, "Hours and employment variation in business cycle theory," Journal of Economic Theory, Vol.1, No.1 /March, 1991, 63-81

Lipsey, R.G, and Carlaw, K (2001), "What Does Total Factor Productivity Measure?", Manuscript, Study Paper Version 02, 1-52.

Long, J.B., and Plosser, C.I., (1983), "Real Business Cycles," The Journal of Political Economy, Vol. 91, No.1 (Feb. 1983), 39-69

Lucas, R.E, 1977, "Understanding Business Cycles," Journal of Monetary Economics, Supplement (1977), Carnegie-Rochester Conference Series, Vol. 1.

Lucas, R.E, 1980, "Methods and Problems in Business Cycle Theory," Journal of Money, Credit and Banking, Vol. 12, No.4, Part 2: Rational Expectations. (Nov. 1980), 696-715
Lucas, R.E (1988), "On the Mechanics of Economic Development", Journal of Monetary Economics, 22, 3-42.

Maddala, G.S and Kim, In-Moo 1998, "Unit Roots, Cointegration and Structural Change," p37 – 146, Cambridge University Press

Mankiw, N.G. (1989), "Real Business Cycles: A New Keynesian Perspective," The Journal of Economic Perspectives, Vol.3, No.3. (Summer 1989), 79-90

Mankiw, N.G, Romer, D, Weil, D.N (1992), "A Contribution to the Empirics of Economic Growth", Quarterly Journal of Economics, Volume 107, Issue 2 (May, 1992), 407-437.

Marchetti, D. J. and Nucci, F., 2005, "Price Stickiness and the Contractionary Effect of Technology Shocks", European Economic Review, 2005, 49(5), 1137 – 1163

McCallum, B.T. (1989), "Real Business Cycles Models," in R.J. Barro (ed.), 'Modern Business Cycles Theory'. Basil Blackwell, Oxford.

McGrattan, E.R. (1994), "The Macroeconomic Effects of Distortionary Taxation", Journal of Monetary Economics, Vol.33, 573-601.

Mendoza, E. (1991), "Real Business Cycles in a Small Open Economy", the American Economic Review, Vol.81, 797-818.

Mikhail. O, 2005, "What Happens After A Technology Shock? A Bayesian Perspective", university of central Florida, Working Paper, 1-30

Minford, P and Sofat, P. (2004), "An Open Economy Real Business Cycle Model for the UK", Manuscript, CASS, 1-80.

Nadiri, M. I, 1970, "Some approaches to the theory and measurement of total factor productivity: a survey", Journal of Economic Literature, Volume 8, Issue 4 (Dec., 1970), 1137 – 1177

Nason, J.M and Cogley, T., 1994, "Testing the implications of long-run neutrality for monetary business cycle models", Journal of Applied Econometrics, Vol. 9, S37 – S70

Ng, S. (1995), "Testing for Unit Roots in Flow Data Sampled at Different Frequencies," Economics Letters, 47, 237-242.

Oulton, N and Srinivasan, S., 2005, "Productivity growth in UK industries, 1970 – 2000: structural change and the role of ICT", The Bank of England's working paper series 259

Oum, T.H; Tretheway, M.W and Zhang, Y. 1991, "A Note on Capacity Utilization and Measurement of Scale Economies", Journal of Business & Economic Statistics, Vol. 9, No.1 (Jan; 1991), 119-123.

Parente, S. L and Prescott, E. C., 2000, Barriers to Riches, MIT Press, Cambridge

Pesavento, E., and Rossi, B., 2004, "Do technology shocks drive hours up or down? A little evidence from an agnostic procedure", Econometrics 0411002, Economics Working Paper, or from (2005) Macroeconomics Dynamics, Cambridge University Press, vol. 9(04), 478 – 488, October, Cambridge Journal 1 – 12

Phelan, C., and Trejos, A., (2000), "The aggregate effects of sectoral reallocation", Journal of Monetary Economics 45, 249 – 268

Phillips, P.C.B., and P. Perron (1988), "Testing for a Unit Root in Time Series Regression," Biometrika, 75, 335-346.

Plosser, C.I., 1989, "Understanding Real Business Cycles," The Journal of Economic Perspectives, Vol.3, No.3 (Summer 1989), 51-77

Prescott, Edward C., 1997, "Needed: A Theory of Total Factor Productivity", Federal Reserve Bank of Minneapolis, Staff Report 242

Ramsey, F.P (1928), "A Mathematical Theory of Saving", Economic Journal, 38, 543-559.

Romer, P.M (1986), "Increasing Returns and Long-run Growth", Journal of Political Economy, 94, 1002 - 1037
Romer, P.M (1990), "Endogenous Technological Change", Journal of Political Change, 98 (5), part 2: S71-S102.
Romer, P.M (1994), "The Origins of Endogenous Growth", Journal of Economic Perspectives, 8 (1): 3 -22.

Rotemberg, J. J and Saloner, G., 1986, "A Super game-theoretic model of price wars during booms", American Economic Review 76, 390 – 407.

Rotemberg, J.J., and Woodford, M., (1995), Dynamic general equilibrium models with imperfectly competitive product markets, in Cooley, T.F., (Ed.), Frontiers of Business Cycle Research. Princeton University Press, Princeton, NJ

Rotemberg, J.J., Woodford, M., (1996), Imperfect competition and the effects of energy price increases on economic activity Journal of Money, Credit, and Banking 28, 550 – 577

Sam Hak Kan Tang, (2002), "The link between growth volatility and technical progress: cross-country evidence", Economics Letters 77 (2002) 335-341

Scherer, F.M. 1982, "Inter-industry Technology Flows and Productivity Growth", The Review of Economics and Statistics, Vol.64, No.4. (Nov; 1982), 627-634.

Schwert, G.W. (1989), Tests for unit roots: A Monte Carlo Investigation," Journal of Business and Economic Statistics, 7, 147-159.

Shapiro, M.D; 1993, "Cyclical Productivity and the Workweek of Capital", the American Economic Review, Vol. 83, No. 2, Papers and proceedings of the Hundred and Fifth Annual Meeting of the American Economic Association. (May, 1993), 229-233

Shapiro, M and Watson, M, 1988, "Sources of Business Cycle Fluctuations", NBER, Macroeconomics Annual 1988, edited by Stanley Fischer, Cambridge, MA: MIT Press

Shapiro, D.M, C. Corrado, P.K. Clark, 1996, "Macroeconomic Implications of Variation in the Workweek of Capital", Brookings Papers on Economic Activity, Vol. 1996, No. 2, 79 – 133.

Shea, J., 1999, "What Do Technology Shocks Do?", in Ben S. Bernanke and Julio J Rotemberg, eds., NBER Macroeconomics Annual, vol.13, Cambridge, MA: MIT Press, 275 – 310
Also (1998) NBER WP 6632, 1 – 26

Sorensen, P.B., and Whitta-Jacobsen, H.J., 2005, "Introducing Advanced Macroeconomics: Growth and business Cycles", McGraw-Hill Companies, London, 397 – 428

Sims, C.A (1980), "Macroeconomics and Reality", Econometrica, 48, 1-48.
Sims, C.A (1972), "Money, Income and Causality", American Economic Review, Vol. 62, No. 4 (Sept, 1972), 540-552.

Solow, R. (1957), "Technical Change and the Aggregate Production Function," Review of Economics and Statistics, 39 (1957), 312-320.
Solow, R.M (1970), "Growth Theory: An Exposition, Oxford University Press, reprinted 1988.
Solow, R.M (1956), "A Contribution to the Theory of Economic Growth", Quarterly Journal of Economics, 70, 65-94.

Swan, T (1956), "Economic Growth and Capital Accumulation", Economic Record 32, 334-361.

Spanos, Aris, 1986, Statistical Foundation of Econometric Modelling, Chapter 3, p.85, Cambridge University Press.

Stadler, G.W. 1994, "Real Business Cycles", Journal of Economic Literature, Vol. XXXII, 1750-1783.

Stiglitz, J. E and Driffill, J 2000, Economics, 647-671, W.W. Norton & Company, New York, London

Taylor, J.B., 1993, "Discretion versus Policy Rules in Practice", Carnegie Rochester Conference Series on Public Policy, 39, 195 – 214.

Thirlwall, A.P, 1994, "Growth and Development with Special Reference to Developing Economies," Macmillan Press, Hong Kong

Uzawa, H 1965, "Optimum Technical Change in an Aggregative Model of Economic Growth", International Economic Review, 6, 18-31.

Vigfusson, R.J., 2004, "The Delayed Response to Technology Shock,: a Flexible Price Explanation", Board of Governors of the Federal Reserve System, International Finance Discussion Papers, N0. 810, 1 – 44

Weitzman, M. L., 1976, "On the Welfare Significance of National Product in a Dynamic Economy", Quarterly Journal of Economics, 90, 156 – 162

Printed in the United States
By Bookmasters